# How to Stitch an

# AMERICAN

# DREAM

*A Story of Family,*
*Faith & the Power of Giving*

# How to Stitch an
# AMERICAN
# DREAM

# Jenny Doan

FOUNDER OF THE MISSOURI STAR QUILT COMPANY

*with* Mark Dagostino

HARPER HORIZON

Published by Harper Horizon, an imprint of HarperCollins Focus LLC.

Book design by Aubrey Khan, Neuwirth & Associates.

Any internet addresses, phone numbers, or company or product information printed in this book are offered as a resource and are not intended in any way to be or to imply an endorsement by Harper Horizon, nor does Harper Horizon vouch for the existence, content, or services of these sites, phone numbers, companies, or products beyond the life of this book.

This is a work of nonfiction. The events and experiences detailed herein are all true and have been faithfully rendered as remembered by the author, to the best of her ability.

ISBN 978-0-7852-5305-1 (eBook)
ISBN 978-0-7852-5303-7 (HC)

Library of Congress Control Number: 2021939622

Printed in the United States of America
21 22 23 24 25  LSC  10 9 8 7 6 5 4 3 2 1

*To my husband and my children,*
*without whom none of this would be possible.*

# Contents

# Contents

# Preface

*A Note from Jenny*

Most of us don't spend a whole lot of time looking back and dwelling on the little details of our own childhood. And I don't think many of us spend much time thinking about the choices we made that led us to where we are in our lives right now, either.

But recently, after my son Alan suggested I ought to write a book, I took a little time to ponder all of that—and *boy* was I surprised at what I found.

It's kind of funny to think about: The things we loved and the things we didn't, the toys we liked to play with and the games we couldn't stand, the projects we were forced to work on in school vs. the hobbies we happily spent hours and hours on at home—they were almost like little fortune tellers, predicting the paths we might want to take, or not take, as we grew up. The lessons our mothers or fathers taught us, or our grandparents or siblings taught us, or the quirky bits of our family histories, or the lessons we learned or tried to ignore in church—all of them seem to connect us to the decisions we end up making down the road, for better or for worse.

Whether we like it or not, the moments we remember, and even some we want to *forget*, all get stitched together over time.

Those separate little pieces form the fabric of our lives, and often help to prepare us for whatever lies ahead.

And sometimes we're not prepared at all! Putting this book together tossed me into an entirely new creative process, and just like with quilting, I learned a whole lot along the way. As you might expect (if you've ever watched one of my tutorials), I remembered a few things in the middle of the process, and changed a few things spontaneously as I went along. I also made more than a few mistakes, and I had a lot of fun while I did it. And while I'm certain this book is not perfect, I am very proud to say that it's *done*.

Who knows, maybe my team and I will start a new YouTube channel to teach some tutorials on book writing someday! Maybe a fresh start when I'm seventy?

All kidding aside, I do hope you enjoy this story of my family—a family that never had a ton, but tried to make the most of everything we had.

Coincidentally, as I was working on this book, our country and the whole world fell into some uncertain times, which may or may not last a whole lot longer than any of us might want. I say "coincidentally" because our family is no stranger to hard times. We founded the Missouri Star Quilt Company right after the stock market crash of 2008. Some of what I'm about to share with you talks about how we navigated through those times and successfully pushed through some other really challenging times long before that, too. We found our strength through those struggles by believing in each other, in our family, in faith, and in the almost magical power of giving—even when it felt like we had nothing left to give.

So today, with a little luck (and of course with the help of my awesome team), I'm hoping that *How to Stitch an American Dream* will inspire you, the way my tutorials might inspire you to try your hand at quilting. By using my family's personal story as the example, what I hope to do is encourage you to take a look back at the fabric of your *own* life; to gain a new perspective, or to unlock your own hidden creativity; to revive a forgotten dream, or maybe even spark a new one. And what I truly hope is that when you take a look at all the scraps and bits and pieces my family managed to pull together to get through life, and to get our business off the ground, you might look inside and remember to believe in you. In *your* dreams. And in your own abilities to do something that you never dared to do before.

It's not too late. It's *never* too late. How do I know?

Because the very idea that I might one day get to share my family and my love of quilting with all of you beautiful people never even entered my mind.

At least, not for the first five decades of my life . . .

*Jenny*

1

# Old Foundations
# & New Pathways

Once upon a time, every mother taught her daughters to sew. Not mine. My mother didn't know how to sew.

Even my grandmother didn't know how to sew.

Yet I distinctly remember "sewing" at a very young age.

I cut tiny pieces out of my mother's old clothing because I needed to make an outfit for my doll. I didn't know how clothes were made, so I put them together however I could: I glued them, stapled them, taped them. In fact, I can't remember a time in my whole life when I wasn't piecing things together.

It is just in my DNA.

Later on in life, I learned that my grandmother's older sisters sewed. They learned to sew from their mother, my great-grandmother, out of necessity, in the late 1800s; and they sewed for their little sister (my grandmother) all the time because she was the youngest of thirteen children.

But some of my great-aunts did much more than sew for the family.

As young women, they found work as seamstresses. And they weren't just your run-of-the-mill seamstresses. They were amazing seamstresses. They sewed for an artist named George Inness Jr. in New York. He was a famous painter whose father had been an even more famous painter of landscapes in the 1800s, and the work they did for him is part of what allowed the family to save enough money to buy a farm in upstate New York in the early 1900s.

Six of my grandmother's thirteen siblings had moved to America from their home country of Sweden by then, and together they chipped in enough money to bring my grandmother, my great-grandmother, my great-grandfather and the rest of the children to America—on the *Titanic*. They booked tickets in steerage because they were still very poor people, but even so, can you imagine how excited they all must have been?

In April of 1912, the family packed up all of their belongings and took a little boat from Sweden to England, where they took a train to Liverpool in order to board that mighty ship. But when they arrived, they found out that the White Star Line had oversold the passage. "We don't have room for all of you," a crew member told my great-grandmother. "But let the boys go. They'll be making history!"

My great-grandmother wasn't having it: "Half of my children are already in America," she said. "I am not splitting up the rest of us. We will all go together or none of us will go at all!"

So, instead of crossing the Atlantic on the largest ship ever built, the family took a smaller ship called the *Cedric*—all the way to America.

Who would have thought that taking a smaller ship would be safer than making the trip on the grandest ship on Earth? But as the world would soon learn, it was. And it's only thanks to that stubborn great-grandmother of mine that my family survived and is here today.

My grandmother was seven years old when they arrived in New York.

Forty-three years later, after getting married and raising two daughters of her own, her husband (my grandfather) died at age fifty-four. And that's what prompted Grandma to come live with us—my mom, my dad, my older sister, my brother, and me—in rural California, shortly after I was born in June of 1957.

In those days, a woman in her fifties or sixties was obviously "too old" to live alone, so my parents set up a room for her in our house. At her age, she also no longer felt comfortable driving a car, but she wanted to work to pay her own way. So, once a week, my parents made the nearly hour-long drive to Pebble Beach to drop her off at a house where she was a housekeeper for a nice man. When she was done, they drove back to Pebble Beach to bring her home, to spend her weekends with us.

That's when Grandma could be found in the kitchen, cooking up something yummy for all of us to eat. ("All of us" would eventually include two younger sisters and another younger brother as well—but that wouldn't be until a few years later.)

I was lucky enough to be raised in a home where *two* Swedish women ruled the kitchen, and they both loved to cook. Everything was made from scratch. If we had breakfast, it might be Swedish pancakes, or homemade jelly on fresh-baked toast, or sweet-smelling cinnamon rolls, but it was often the dessert from the night before. During the week, my dad would get up to drive us to school at 7:00 a.m. and he would say, "Grab yourself a piece of cake" or whatever was left over. We had the best dang dessert-breakfasts ever!

I loved using my hands and making things as a kid, and I always wanted to help in the kitchen, but with both of them cooking there just wasn't a place for me. I had to find another outlet.

By the time I was ten years old, it seemed like all the kids were getting into 4-H, including my friend Annette. We used to spend our school lunch breaks reading Nancy Drew novels together. We didn't even really talk about them. We'd just sit together on the grass and read, and that was enough. Annette's mom, Mrs. Violini, happened to be a 4-H teacher, and she became one of my favorites, but it was another 4-H teacher, Mrs. Long, who first taught me how to sew. An apron was the first project we made in 4-H. It was just a half-a-yard of fabric with a casing sewn over it. She taught me how to put a string through it and squinch it up and tie it around my waist. *Done*. It was so easy! I felt like I had really accomplished something. I still remember holding it up and thinking, *Wow! I* made *this. I made this apron!*

I was hooked.

Over the next three years, many wonderful teachers taught me how to make curtains and placemats and all kinds of clothing. 4-H was a wealth of information for a kid who wanted to create.

When I turned fourteen, my grandma gave me my very first sewing machine for Christmas: a Swedish Viking Husqvarna.

While my grandmother did not follow in the footsteps of her much-older sisters, she wasn't completely helpless when it came to working with a needle and thread. Her creative outlet was embroidery. She loved to embroider flowers, and my job was to cut up the family's old denim jeans into squares for her to embroider on. There was a time when she would make one of her embroidered squares every day, or every day-and-a-half.

Then she handed me stacks of those squares and asked, "Could you sew six of these together? I want to send them to your aunt Ingie." I did what she asked, and she checked my work, then she handed me back the six stitched-together squares and said, "Just hem the edge so it's not all ragged," and I'd hem the edge, and we'd send it off. She would send them to other relatives and friends too.

I didn't realize at the time that I was helping my grandmother to make little quilts.

I didn't even know what quilting was.

In my mind, I was just sewing some embroidered squares together for Grandma.

Before learning to sew, my big job at home was to clean the bathrooms. So this felt like quite the promotion!

It wasn't long before I was sewing all my own clothes. That was partly out of necessity, because I was already five feet nine and we couldn't find things that fit me in any of the stores. But whenever anybody in the family needed something mended or sewn, they would come to me. One time my little brother came running in begging, "Jenny, I ripped my pants again. Can you please sew these up?"

"Yeah, sure," I said, "but I'm usin' the thread I have on here, and it's pink!"

Of course, I changed out the thread before I did it, but I had so much fun teasing him.

———

Genealogy was a big thing in our little corner of California in the 1960s, and my mom loved it. One of her favorite things to do was to take us all on picnics at the cemetery, where she would send us on scavenger hunts. She made up a whole long list of things for us to find and then sent us kids buzzing around looking for them.

"Today I want you to find a tombstone that has your name on it," she'd say. Or, "Go look for the tombstone of a child." Other times it was, "Find a tombstone with an etching of a lamb on it," or "See if you can find the grave of a soldier from World War I."

I'm pretty sure none of us kids were ever afraid of cemeteries because she made those trips so much fun.

Later on in life, Mom opened a little shop in a room in the front of the house where she sold genealogy books and supplies. She did some genealogical research for other people. She turned her passion into something that brought in a little income, which I thought was pretty cool.

My mom painted our own genealogy chart on the wall too. And for every long-lost relative who had a birthdate on that wall, she would bake a cake and throw them a birthday party. Mom *loved* to bake. In fact, years later, on one of the first times my future husband, Ron, came over to my mother's house, she happened to be throwing one of those parties.

He sure was surprised when he walked in.

"Whose birthday is it?" he asked.

I looked up and scanned the wall, pointing to the name of the person whose date of birth matched: "Joseph B. Long's," I replied.

"Who is he?" Ron asked.

"Oh, some guy on the wall. We have birthday parties for these people all the time."

After he got his first bite of that chocolate cake, Ron decided my mom's house was a pretty great place to be!

(I've included my mother's chocolate sheet-cake recipe at the end of the book!)

My dad was born in 1931, and his father was a builder. When he was growing up, his family would live in a tent while they built a house, then they'd live in the house until they sold the house, and then they would move out and move back to the tent to do it all again. So, at seventeen, my dad joined the Air Force. He didn't want to live in tents anymore.

After the Air Force, he continued his no-tent lifestyle by becoming one of the first boys in our family to go to college. Dad was attending Cal Poly in San Luis Obispo in 1957 when I was born. After college he became a chemist and worked for the Smucker Company for most of his life. But his true love was building, and he regularly referred to me as his helper.

I loved working with my dad. I shared his passion for being outside and building things. I liked the feel of the tools, and the smell of the dirt when we were digging. And I absolutely loved watching something come from nothing.

Dad taught me how to hammer a nail, to hand-saw boards, and to build things out of whatever materials we could gather. He showed me how to make things from the scraps and pieces that other people might just throw away. He also taught me how to fix things when they were broken. It didn't matter to him even one tiny bit that I was a girl, and it all came pretty easy to me.

For the most part, everything came pretty easy to me. I worked hard at what made me happy, and I carried that with me. Both Mom and Dad still tell stories of me waking up singing, all excited about the possibilities of the day and the adventures we were going to have.

My positive attitude and easygoing nature didn't always sit well with others. Like the time my older sister got a bike for her tenth birthday. She was mad because she tried and tried and couldn't figure out how to ride it. I had never ridden a bike before, but at six years old I climbed on her bike and figured it out. I started pedaling and took off riding. I came back smiling and offered to teach her how to do it, and she was *furious* at me. She ran inside crying to our mom.

After my mother calmed her down, she took me aside and said, "Jenny, you didn't do anything wrong. But what I told your sister might apply to you someday, and I want you to always remember this: 'Do the best you can and be happy for those who can do it better.'"

Years later I wrote that line down in a journal and it became one of the things that I have lived by and have taught my children: *Do the best you can and be happy for those who can do it better.*

The lesson our mom taught us that day was a good one, and I'm pretty sure it's a lesson she picked up from the teachings of our church.

When we were all pretty young, some missionaries from the Church of Jesus Christ of Latter-day Saints knocked on my parents' door—and my dad let them in. From what I understand, my parents had tried going to different churches and tried to find the answers to some of life's big questions elsewhere, but they never quite found what they were looking for. The message those missionaries delivered must've been a good one, because my parents decided to join their church.

The particular branch of the church my parents joined didn't have many members in California in the 1960s. They didn't even have a church building to gather in near us. So, before anyone had the funds to build a proper church, we used to meet above a bar in Soledad. We kids would go upstairs and help clean up beer bottles and push the tables aside before we could have our services.

That's where I learned that a church wasn't about a building at all, and that faith could be found just about anywhere. This church was about people, and community, and helping each other. It was about learning to be a good person—the kind of person who values family, and tries to do good things for others, and tries to do good things in the world.

It's funny to think I learned all that by going to church above a bar. But life's like that, isn't it? Full of beauty found in unexpected places.

———

When I was ten years old, we moved to a big-old, run-down Victorian in Spreckels, a little town just about twenty miles east of Monterey Bay, near the bigger town of Salinas. Spreckels had four streets. It was a *very* small community with a small K–8 school, where the biggest excitement was learning my first swear word. (I'm not going to tell you which one!)

My parents got a good deal on the house because it needed to be fixed up, and my dad knew how to do it. He used to go help tear down old houses in the area so we could recycle the pieces and use them in ours. We were basically using what other people saw as scraps to turn our own house into something beautiful.

The toughest job was probably removing old foundations, because in those days a lot of foundations in that part of the country were made of bricks. We'd have to break 'em apart and load all those heavy bricks into my dad's truck. Then he would pay us kids a penny a brick to clean off the old cement. All the hard work was worth it, though, because at home we used those bricks to make the most beautiful pathways in our yard.

Like I said, the things I loved were not the typical girl things. Maybe I was a little ahead of my time that way. But my parents raised me to believe that anybody could do anything.

I even learned how to shoot a BB gun. I figured, "If a boy could do it, I could do it too."

Still, my mom did keep strict modesty rules for us girls. Our skirts had to be a certain length, and we had to wear dresses with nylons to church, even when it was hot. And we certainly weren't allowed to wear white after Labor Day. Later in life I would learn that a lot of the rules she taught us weren't "rules" at all. It was just a matter of her trying to raise us the best way she knew how at the time, which was the same way she had been raised. Things had to be done a certain way, and everything had to be "proper," which was very in line with that whole generation's *Leave It to Beaver*–style of parenting. I didn't agree with a lot of it, but I didn't hold any of it against her. I just decided that I would do things differently when I grew up.

Trying to raise kids in the 1960s in California wasn't easy for my parents, but it seemed especially hard on Mom. Before she had children, she was an English major, and she loved poetry. She shared poetry with us kids all the time. Once, she gave me a poetry book, and she handwrote this message in the front of it:

> *I'm as uncomfortable in your four-letter society*
> *as you are in my white-glove one.*

Everything was changing so fast, and the chances of our family ever being the "perfect" one she and my father imagined were slim.

Like when my unmarried sister got pregnant.

At first my siblings and I didn't know what had happened. Our sister went away, and no one would tell us where she went. Later we learned that my parents arranged for her to have her baby in a home far away from us, because that's what people did in those days.

I was still trying to put all the pieces of this together in my mind when, one day, my dad and I were busy sanding the floor of our old house together, and the phone rang. He got up and took the call while I kept working, then he came down and went back to sanding. He was on his knees, and I was near him, helping him—when all of a sudden he leaned over and started sobbing. He covered his face in his hands and he wept.

I did not know what that conversation was about. I didn't know who he had spoken with. I just knew that my dad's heart was breaking over whatever he'd been told. And seeing him cry like that? A little girl remembers such things.

I knew I couldn't fix it. I knew I couldn't make it better. But I wanted to, with all my heart.

**2**

# Breaking Barriers & Jumping In

I entered my teenage years in 1970, just a year after the Apollo moon landing, at the dawn of a brand-new decade, when the whole world seemed to be opening up to new possibilities.

Most people thought I was a lot older than I was, mostly because of my height. In reality, I was a kid at heart. (I think I still am!) My brain always went straight to, "If it's fun, we should do it!" And I was pretty slow to think about consequences, which led me to do some pretty crazy stuff.

Like in 1971, when an older boy I knew had a car that I liked. That car looked like fun, so I asked him one day, "Can I drive your car?" And to my surprise he said yes.

I laughed at him at first. "I'm fourteen! I don't have a license!" I said.

But he said, "I'll show you."

And he did.

Once I got the hang of it, I drove his car right onto the highway. And it *was* fun, until we were on our way home. Two cars ahead of us, there was an older man driving, and I guess he slowed down to turn without using his blinker. The car behind him slammed on his brakes, and all of a sudden I heard boom, boom, *boom*, and my face smacked into the steering wheel.

My friend and I looked at each other in shock.

"Are you okay?" he asked.

"Yeah. No. Maybe? I don't know," I said. I was pretty tough, but my face hurt and my head was throbbing.

"I'm so sorry," I said.

"It's okay. It happened so fast. It could happen to anyone," he said.

Everyone got out of their cars and checked to see that nobody was seriously injured, and we exchanged phone numbers. No one asked how old I was or bothered to check if I had a license. They probably saw my face turning black-and-blue and were more concerned that I got home safely.

My face wasn't the worst part. Neither was the shock of what had happened.

Somehow I had to tell my dad what I had done. My friend drove me home and the whole way I stared out the passenger-side window, thinking about how upset my dad was going to be, and how I never wanted to make him upset.

When I got there, he took one look at me and knew something bad had happened. I had no choice but to tell him the whole story. And I did. Through tears.

"I'm sorry, Dad. I'm so sorry. I won't ever do it again," I said. Then I waited for him to say something.

After a long silence, he looked at me and said, "Well, thank goodness you're okay. But I hope you learned a lesson."

That was it. No grounding. No big punishment.

I guess the bottom line was he already knew that teenagers do stupid things sometimes, and maybe he was grateful it wasn't a whole lot worse. Or maybe he figured my bruised face was punishment enough? I'm not sure. He didn't even seem to be all that upset—until he called my friend to find out what the damages were to his car. That's when he picked up his checkbook and shook it at me with a look on his face that said, "Do you know what this is gonna cost me?"

I felt so terrible about disappointing my dad. I'm not sure if that was the first time, but unfortunately it wouldn't be the last.

By the time I reached high school, I was having a lot of fun making my own clothes, following store-bought patterns. Many of the modern hippie-clothes of the day were very easy to make and looked great for a quarter of what it would have cost to buy them at a clothing store. I'm still surprised that my mother let me out of the house in some of those short skirts and flowy dresses, but I think she appreciated my talent and the money I was saving her.

I also think there was a part of her that really enjoyed watching me express my creativity.

One of my mom's favorite poets, interestingly, was e.e. cummings—a poet who tended to break a lot of old rules about poetry and language, and who was all about expressing individuality. She shared his poetry with us on many occasions, and in high school I took a little inspiration from him and started signing my name with a lowercase "j."

I wrote "jenny" at the top of every paper and felt pretty proud about doing my own thing—until one of my teachers said I could not do that.

"You need to write your name with a capital 'J,'" she insisted.

"Well, e.e. cummings doesn't write his name with a capital 'E,'" I said.

"He's a published author," she replied. "When you're a published author, you can choose how you write your name."

(I guess that means she would approve now, and I can sign this book as "jenny"?)

"It's *my* name and I'll write it however I *want!*" I argued back.

The teacher was not having it. It was not the way things were supposed to be done. She said, "You do not get to take shortcuts and make up the rules. There is a right way to do things, and you will do things right."

I got detention for talking back, and they called my mom into the office.

As expected, she was pretty angry when she got there. She looked at me and said, "Jenny, you do not show disrespect to your teachers." She told me to apologize for that right there, and I did. But then she turned and looked straight at the teacher and said, "Now, my daughter is going to write her name any way she pleases."

I was stunned.

And can you imagine my teacher's surprise?

It's not always easy to love your mom when you're a teenager, but on that day? I had the coolest mom in the world.

Seeing her stand up for me like that—I've never forgotten it.

It also wasn't the first or last time I pushed a few boundaries in my high school. In those days, there were silly rules like girls weren't allowed to take woodshop. It wasn't even an option. But after working with tools and building things with my dad my whole life, that rule didn't make any sense to me. So I fought to change it, and I won! I became the first girl in my school who was ever allowed to enroll in woodshop. I still had a hard time getting close to any of the table saws or other heavy machines because the boys would step in and say, "Oh, let me do that for you." But by that time, I was starting to appreciate a little attention from boys, so I didn't really mind it.

I turned sixteen in 1973, the same year the Vietnam War came to an end, *Roe v. Wade* went to the Supreme Court, and Billie Jean King beat Bobby Riggs in the Battle of the Sexes tennis match on TV. Society was changing quickly, and so was I.

**AFTER I TURNED SIXTEEN,** my mom and dad helped me with a room makeover. We sanded and refinished the floors, painted the walls white—and my mom secretly made me a chicken-scratch quilt in bright green. Chicken-scratch was a type of cross-stitch done over big one-inch gingham squares, and she used white yarn. It had prairie points all around the edges.

I already mentioned that my mom didn't sew. Never had. But she went to a friend who helped her put it together. It was fascinating to me that she would dedicate so much time doing something she had never done before, just for me.

I got my driver's license at the same time the boys in school started to catch up to my height, and I'll admit I was definitely a little boy crazy. I loved going to dances, dating, and going to the beach. I didn't have my own car yet, but I had friends who did, and we gathered groups of girls and guys together to pile in their cars and go to the beach. No matter how crazy something seemed, if it sounded like fun, I was all-in!

So when my favorite teacher, Mr. Green, who had put me in his advanced choral group as one of the youngest members ever, asked the group if we wanted to go to Russia, I immediately said yes!

Between my sophomore and junior year, our choral group was invited to be a part of Ensembles East, a monthlong tour that would take us to sing all over Eastern Europe, long before the Berlin Wall came down.

It was a chance of a lifetime. My parents agreed to let me go, but they said I had to pay for half of it. That sounded great to me! *No problem,* I thought. I was such a go-getter, I went out and worked in the celery fields and earned half the money myself. My parents paid the other half, just as they'd promised. Then a nice lady in our neighborhood gave me some spending money, out of the blue, without asking for anything in return. I couldn't believe it! She said she was excited for me to go and see the world!

Next thing I knew, we were standing in Red Square. In Moscow. We were allowed to go right inside this big building to see the preserved body of former Soviet leader Vladimir Lenin encased in glass. Yet there were armed guards on some of the streets, and certain streets we weren't allowed to go down. There were buildings riddled with bullet holes. One of the kids in our group had a camera hanging off of his belt, and he got taken to the police station for questioning.

We were warned that if we went outside with jeans on, we'd be approached by people wanting us to sell them on the black market. "Don't do that," Mr. Green told us.

We didn't have cell phones and apps back then to help us with translations, or currency exchange, or conversions, and none of us really understood the money. It all looked like play money to us. So a few of us chipped in and bought a kilo of chocolate. We didn't realize that a kilo was 2.2 pounds! It was too much for us to eat, so we gave half of it to the maid at the hotel—and she broke down and sobbed. A chunk of chocolate that we were all laughing over and enjoying just for fun meant so much to this woman that she *cried*.

I would never forget that.

In Romania, we saw huge haystacks in the fields, and then women in dresses with black stockings who were shoveling the hay up into those giant piles. It felt like we were inside the pages of a storybook. We saw a whole family riding down the road on a big tractor, and realized it was probably the only vehicle they owned; the only way they could all get around, to work and school and everything.

That one trip gave all of us so much new perspective on the world, and a much deeper appreciation for everything we had at home. Mr. Green did that for me. For all of us. Not only was he a great choral teacher, but he was funny and kind and really cared about us. He watched out for us, and he made himself available to us if we needed to talk. He didn't just teach us technically about music, he taught us the joy of music and a love of singing and the beauty of working together in a group. And, on top of it all, he took us on an adventure of a lifetime.

Isn't it amazing what one really good teacher can do?

---

After that trip, I started taking charge of my own life. I got a job, and right after my eighteenth birthday I went out and got my own apartment. With roommates, because there was no way to afford a place on my own. I also bought my own car and paid for that myself too. My dad had to co-sign on the loan, because in those days a young woman wasn't seen as credit-worthy if she wasn't married. But still, that car—a used 1972 yellow Pinto—was *mine*.

Dating was all kinds of fun for me. I liked the chase. I'd set my eyes on boys just to see if I could get them interested, and then I'd let them go. But by the end of high school, I was going steady with a boy who seemed like the kind of boyfriend a girl could marry, which I assumed was the next step now that I was a grown-up. There was only one problem: he went away on a two-year mission for our church, which left me all alone.

It wasn't long before another guy caught my eye. He was slightly older, new in town, and new to our church. When one of my roommates started dating his best friend, we started dating too. The two of us girls were having a whole lot of fun with these guys when out of the blue she told me that they had decided to get married. They asked me and my new boyfriend to drive to Reno with them and stand up as their witnesses, and of course I jumped in and said, "Yes! Of course! It'll be so much fun!"

Before anyone could change their minds, we piled into a car and drove to Nevada.

The whole adventure was so romantic and special that, once we got there, they dared the two of us to get married too.

And we *did*.

I got married. On a dare. In Reno. At nineteen years old.

It was pure teenage-brain in action.

My mother and father were shocked and heartbroken when I called them with the news. And, looking back now, I can't even imagine myself doing it. At the time I figured we would probably end up getting married anyway, so why not?

But I was about to learn a lot of hard lessons, really fast.

# Love Lessons
# & Gratitude

On Sundays, even when I was young and impulsive and newly married to a man I barely knew, I still went to church. And one time I overheard an older lady there who was griping on and on about her husband. He had retired and was home underfoot all the time. I had no wisdom and no experience under my belt, so I spoke right up and said to her: "Well, the alternative is he could be dead!"

She looked at me so fast. Right away I knew I probably shouldn't have said that, so I apologized and then said, "Well, you don't seem to like him too much."

The bottom line is she *did* like him. She loved him. But she had lived her whole life in a domain that was hers, and now she had to share it. That was her new challenge in life.

And I was about to learn for myself just how difficult new challenges can be.

---

This isn't easy to talk about. I don't like to talk about it. But many of us get divorces. A lot of us have that in common. So here goes!

I went into my first marriage thinking it was going to be great. I wasn't worried about how spontaneous we were. I thought it was all going to be wonderful. I told myself, *It's going to work, and everything's going to be roses every day!* But a good marriage isn't like that, you know?

Setting aside the sort of crazy way it started, I believed wholly that I could figure this marriage thing out. I also had every expectation that it was going to be *fun*. Maybe even romantic. Why shouldn't it be?

But almost right away I had a feeling that maybe I'd made a mistake.

The truth is, I really had no idea what I had gotten myself into.

I had no idea that my new husband's father was abusive, and that he might follow in those footsteps. I didn't know anything about abuse. I thought all marriages were like my parents'.

My dad was always so loving to my mom. He was kind and present and fun and a really good husband, and that's the only kind of husband-example I knew.

Pretty early on, my new husband and I moved away from home and away from my family, and things got pretty wild. I didn't go to parties or hang out with people who did drugs, and I had never been around anything like that. So I didn't understand a lot of what was happening. I just knew it wasn't good.

When I asked about it, he grew angry. We argued. He yelled. And the arguments kept getting worse.

The first time he hit me, I was so shocked, I looked him in the eyes and said, "Does that make you feel like a big man?"

He hauled off and hit me again.

When the pain and shock wore off a little bit, I thought, *Okay, that didn't work. That did not work at all.*

He had a way of spinning things around and blaming me, and then I would blame myself. I felt like maybe I had egged him on because he said I was a "mouthy woman." And I started to doubt myself. I wondered if he was right. It was true that if someone said something to me, it was in my nature to say some-thing right back.

All I can say is this: When you are in the deep muck of it all, and somebody who is supposed to love you is telling you over and over that it is all your fault, you just start to believe that. And you get really lost.

In those days we didn't have the research, the advocates, and the information that is available to young women who find themselves in these situations today. And in church we were taught that our job was to love and support our husbands; that through that love, everything would get better. Me, being a strong woman, I believed I could do that. I believed that I could try harder and figure it out. I could *fix this.* I'd been fixing things my whole life.

But that wasn't what happened.

There were a couple of really dark years during that time that aren't easy to talk about to this day. But then, I got pregnant.

The day my first baby, Natalie, came into this world, my heart just about burst open with more love than I could have ever imagined. That little baby was everything to me and somehow, her sweet smile brought me back to life. Not only did I have somebody who reciprocated love, but it was what I really wanted, and what made me happy deep down in my heart.

Unfortunately it was not what my husband wanted, and my really bad marriage suddenly got a whole lot worse.

One night, when he had one of his sudden, explosive fits, I was holding Natalie in my arms—and he knocked me over the couch. The screams of that tiny, scared baby went right through my heart, and in that moment, reality hit me harder than he ever did.

I knew God would want me to protect this little baby.

I decided that I needed some time to figure it out. I said to him, "I think I'm gonna go visit my family." And I loaded Natalie in the car and drove the six hours back to Spreckels.

After a couple of weeks I called him, and I said, "I think I'm gonna come home. I really miss you."

These days there's a name for that sort of thing. It's called *trauma bonding*. But back then, people assumed we were just going through a "rough patch." Something we would "get over" or "get through."

I was alone at my mom's with this beautiful little blonde baby, *our* baby, and I loved her more than I loved anything in my life. And I was still living in the land of wishful thinking. I still wanted to believe that he could love us and be the husband and father that we needed him to be. So I prayed on it every day. But when I called him again to tell him I wanted to come home, he said, "Don't."

"Why?" I asked.

"Well, I'm really busy at work," he said. "I feel like you need to see your family more."

I was definitely happy to share Natalie with my family. They loved her so much. So I stayed. Another couple of weeks passed, and I started to feel sick. It got so bad that I went to see my doctor. "There's something wrong," I said. "I'm just so tired. I feel like I need a shot of caffeine or iron or something. I can't even function."

The doctor ran some tests and came in and said, "Well, you're pregnant."

"What? I'm still nursing. I was told you couldn't get pregnant when you're nursing. How could I be?"

"Well," he said, "it happens."

I left the office in a daze.

I called my husband again and said, "I really need to talk to you. I feel like I should come home now." But he still didn't want me to. He made all these excuses. I had to tell him the news and didn't want to tell him over the phone. So I put Natalie in the car and drove back to San Diego.

When I got there and opened the door to our house, the first thing I noticed was the mess. There were full ashtrays and empty beer bottles everywhere. I held Natalie tightly in my arms, not wanting to put her down, as I tried not to vomit from the heavy smell of the cigarettes and some strange perfume. Then I noticed the clothing. A woman's clothing. It was tossed all over. It was on my couch and on the chairs and on the floor, and even on my bed.

It was a total betrayal.

I stood there frozen as Natalie cried to get out of my arms. I cleared off her high chair, strapped her safely in, and gave her some Cheerios. Then I picked up the phone and called him at work.

"So, I'm at home," I said, "and I don't know who these cigarettes belong to, or who these beer bottles belong to, or whose clothing this is, but none of it belongs to me."

"Why are you home?" he snapped at me.

He wasn't missing me or missing the baby. He was angry that I came home. And when he found out that I was pregnant? He was furious.

I don't know that it all happened on that day, but I do know it all happened fairly quickly. He told me he wanted a divorce.

For three years I had been stewing in some irrational idea that everything was my fault, and that somehow I could try harder and fix it and make it work. But I couldn't fix this. The problem was never me. At one point early on he had admitted that he was afraid of what he would "do" with a family because of what his abusive father had done to him. And now we knew.

So what next?

I did what I knew how to do: I prayed. I went to my church and I asked God to help me.

In those days, the perspective of the older generations was, *You made this bed, you lie in it.* You're on your own, you know? Going back to visit my family for a few weeks was one thing, but there was no going back to stay. I was sure of it. My parents wouldn't have it.

In the moment, I couldn't see a way out of my predicament. But I did know that I could trust in God. And God came through: some people from my church connected me and Natalie with a new place to live in San Diego, so I could figure out my next steps.

I was alone, with no job, no husband, a baby, another baby on the way, and a whole lot to figure out. But when I finally swallowed the reality of it all, I realized that being hurt, scared, lost, and lonely was bad—but I could also focus on being grateful. I was *grateful* the marriage was over. I was grateful that I'd never have to hold my breath again and worry what was going to happen next. I was grateful for my first beautiful little baby, Natalie, who I had been given the honor of being a mother to, and for the precious little baby that was on the way.

I was grateful that I wouldn't have to worry about our safety anymore.

It's times like these when we often get closer to God. And I did. Every day I would pray: "Heavenly Father, help me to get through this day. Help me to be a good mom to these babies. Help me to make good choices. Help me to find the strength to forgive, and to find my path. Help me to know what it is I should do."

And then one day, an answer came. I woke up with a very strong feeling: I needed to call my dad.

"Dad," I said, "I have everything set up here so I can stay. I even have a place to live, but I had a feeling—and I really think that I'm supposed to come home."

He was silent for a moment, and then he said, softly, "I think so too."

I cried when I hung up the phone. I was so, so grateful for my dad.

The next week he got on a plane, flew down to San Diego, and rented a truck. We loaded up my stuff and drove home.

The fact that he was willing to come get me meant so much.

When my dad came to pick me up, he looked me in the eyes with such pain, and he said, "What has happened to you? You used to be so confident, so sure of yourself, so outspoken, so strong."

What *had* happened to me?

I would wrestle with that question for a long time.

And learning to trust again? That was not going to be easy.

---

After we got home, I threw myself into the arms of the church and found so much love and support in our community.

For the first couple of months it wasn't obvious to everyone that I was pregnant, because we wore our clothes big and loose in those days. Hardly anyone noticed. That was a good thing, on the one hand, but it also meant I didn't have many people I could talk to about what I was feeling.

To help me get through it all, and to make sense of it all, I began writing in a journal that summer.

I still have that journal, and all of my journals, tattered and worn, sitting on a shelf in my home.

I made my first entry on July 7, 1979:

*I am starting this journal during a period of my life when my feelings need an outlet for expression. As of now I'm living with my parents, with my child, Natalie, who is 14 months old. I am pregnant, due to deliver on August 3rd, approximately three weeks from now. I am living with my folks due to the fact that my husband and I are separated after nearly three years of marriage and almost two children. He's decided to live a life completely contrary to that of our beliefs. He doesn't want anything to do with his family or the church. So at age 22 I am left with two children to raise. I love these children more than life itself, and I feel so sorry for [him] when he realizes what he has given up. He will really be sorry. I know beyond a shadow of a doubt that everything that happens, happens for a reason, and also that God will never give you more than you can handle. I have gained such a strong testimony of the gospel and the love of the Lord for each one of us. I feel that my attitude toward all that has happened is good. I can't be sad all of my life. I must go on. I am trying to do that as much as I can. The hardest part is that I need companionship so badly. I don't like being alone, but I suppose everything can be gotten used to. We must really trust the Lord and let him lead our lives. Only then can we be sure of making the right decision.*

# Second Chances & Soda Fountain Dreams

The first time I met Ronald Doan was at a church dance. I was just seventeen.

I walked in looking like a full-blown wild hippie, with the sandals, the long hair, the flowy dress, and Ron showed up in pleated bell-bottom pants with a cuff, a navy blue blazer with golden buttons, and a starched navy shirt with a white tie. His motorcycle-riding best friend introduced us, and I said, "Well, aren't you looking dapper?"

Ron was so shy that all he said was, "Hi." And I remember thinking, *Is that it? Is there more there?* But that was all he had to say to me.

At the time, Ron was twenty-one, and that seemed really old to me. When you're in high school, anyone out of high school seemed old, but from the way he dressed he seemed as old as my parents, so I didn't give him another thought. I knew he rode motorcycles, just like his friend did, and I heard at some point that he was leaving on a two-year mission for our church. But that was all I knew about him.

So imagine my surprise when I came back to Spreckels (at age 22), and one of the first people I ran into at church was Ron Doan.

I said, "Hi, Ron. Good to see you. How are you?"

"Hi, Jenny. I'm good. I just got back yesterday."

"Oh wow. I just got back myself. How was your mission?"

To my surprise, this formerly shy guy started talking. He told me all about what he'd been up to, and where he'd traveled to, and my first thought was: *Wow! You are actually speaking in full sentences! Something must have magically changed you.*

After talking and laughing real easily together for a while, I teased him: "How come you never asked me out?"

"Because you were always with somebody else," he said.

So I teased him again: "Well, how do you think they got there?" I said.

He shrugged his shoulders.

"They asked!" I said. And he blushed.

I didn't know it then, but it turns out Ronald Doan thought I was all-that-and-a-bag-of-chips.

**RON:** I don't know what it was about her. I was just drawn to her. I was drawn to her from the day we met. She was a beautiful young woman. But it was much more than that. She was always so happy, and outgoing, and everybody loved to be around her. She was beautiful inside and out.

A few days later, my car stopped working. I didn't know what I was going to do, since I had no money to get it fixed. But when I saw Ron at church again, I said, "You know what? I don't know if I can even ask you this, but I know you fix motorcycles. I'm having a little problem with my car. Do you think you could come look at it?"

I offered to feed him dinner if he would, and he didn't hesitate. "Yeah," he said. "I'll come."

He came over to my parents' house the very next day. Natalie was toddling around as I sat out there on the curb and talked to him while he looked at my car. And he said, "Well, you have a gas hose that isn't good," and he fixed it on the spot.

After dinner, Ron said, "I'd love to come back and see you again."

"I'd really like that," I said.

Later that week I wrote this in my journal:

*July 21, 1979*

*Things have been going really well and as good as can be under the circumstances. I now have 13 days until I am due. I'm getting really anxious to have this baby. I have secured a place to live. It's a little house in need of a few repairs, right in Spreckels, next to the gas station on the boulevard. It's good to know that I have a place to go to. I can't move in yet as the repairs have to be made. The other night one of the guys I knew from church came out to do a favor and fix my car. His name is Ron. He has just returned from a mission in Indiana. He is 25 years old and such a nice guy. He stayed after he fixed my car, and we talked for about three hours. It was really fun. (He might have promise.)*

Ron showed up the next day after work, and he came the next day and the next day too.

My mother had a couch in the family room, and it had three cushions. And I would sit on one end and he would sit on the other end, and we would talk and talk about our days.

My mother said, "When that middle cushion goes down, you two are in trouble."

I really didn't see it that way. I thought we were just friends, but as we talked, he kept coming up with these stories of times we'd been together.

"Do you remember that time when I took a whole carload of kids to the beach, and I let you have the front seat and you fed me a po' boy sandwich?" he asked.

"No," I said. "Did we talk to each other? Did we spend time at the beach?"

"No, not really," he said.

"Well, did you get my letter?" he asked me.

"What letter?"

"The one I sent when I was on my mission."

"No."

I never received it, and I could hardly imagine why he'd even sent it. But to my surprise, I discovered that Ron had all sorts of memories of me.

**RON:** Racing motorcycles was my thing in those days, and every weekend my friend and I would go out to Salinas and ride our bikes up in the hills all day long. That was our practice and training for years, and it was so much fun. We would spend all day doing that, while my friend's sister-in-law, Diane, would go to church. Then she would come back and fix us dinner. At the end of the day we'd all sit around and play Parcheesi or other games, and she'd talk with us about religion.

Sometimes we would babysit for Diane and her husband, and their youngest one always wanted me to read her bedtime stories out of the Book of Mormon. So I started reading the Book of Mormon when I was babysitting, and I just thought it was interesting. I grew up going to a First Southern Baptist

Church. My dad was from Texas. My mom was from Arkansas. So this was the first exposure to another religion that I'd ever really had.

I was twenty-one when I was baptized, and it was right after that when I met Jenny at the church dance. Like I said, there was just something so special about her. But I didn't know what to say to her. In those days if you put me on a motorcycle I was okay, but talk to me face-to-face, no.

I saw her many times after that, at dances and other social functions. But I'm not a dancer, and she never seemed to notice me, so I admired her from afar. I hardly ever talked to her. But I can still tell you the details of each and every time we were in the same place at the same time.

That memory of driving her to the beach and her feeding me the sandwich, that's a big one. I would never have eaten a po'boy sandwich if she wasn't the one feeding it to me. But I also drove her and some mutual friends other places other times. I had a big van that I used to carry my race bikes in, and I had it customized inside, with paneling, and I waxed all the seats down. I'd always offer to drive people places. So we'd take off and stop and everybody'd be sliding off the seats, and I remember Jenny laughing and laughing and saying, "Do it again!" So I'd do it again just to hear her laugh. I loved the way she laughed. I still do.

I was still racing motorcycles when I decided to go on a mission for the church at twenty-three. The missions are a two-year commitment, and you have to pay your own way. I knew my parents wouldn't support me, so I sold all my motorcycles and my van to pay for it.

When I found out that God called me on a mission to Indianapolis, Indiana, the Racing Capital of the World? I thought, *God* does *love me!*

Two years later, when Jenny walked into church again the very weekend I came back, my heart stopped. I thought if all I ever got to do was stand next to her and look at her it might be enough for me. But then she walked over and *talked* to me . . .

I also noticed that he wasn't bothered one bit by the fact that I had a daughter, or that I was about to have a baby any day. He got right down on the floor to play with Natalie, with no hesitation at all. Just like I did. He thought it was cool! And he seemed very happy when I told him I was in the process of getting a divorce.

*July 25, 1979*

*Ron comes over quite regularly, and he is or seems to be very interested in me. It's very hard for me as I am still legally married, and I can't do any chasing on my own. But believe me, I am in no rush to get back into that boat (marriage). I am going to be sure this time that I make the right choice. Ron is really good with Natalie, and he is such a comfort to me. I felt differently about him from the first, but I'm not sure what different means. I hope I have this baby soon . . .*

Just a few days after I wrote that, we took Natalie to the Dennis the Menace Park in Monterey so she could play. Everyplace we went, people thought we were a family. I mean, why wouldn't they? I was pregnant, and Natalie was fourteen months old.

Later that night, my water broke. My mom took me to the hospital.

We walked in at 1:00 a.m., and my second baby girl, Sarah, arrived at 1:20.

I called Ron just after sunrise, and he came right over to see us. He was one of the first ones there. It melted my heart to share the love of my beautiful new baby with someone who truly wanted to see her, and hold her, and be there for me.

SHORTLY AFTER SARAH WAS BORN, I moved into the little duplex I'd found. It was tiny, but I didn't care. I fiercely wanted to be independent and on my own, you know? And I watched as my dad and Ron worked together to build a little fence around the yard for Natalie, so she could go outside and play.

My parents adored Ron. Baby Sarah adored him right away. And Natalie loved him too.

Natalie was a quiet, cuddly little girl. Like all new moms, I really didn't think anybody could take care of her the way I could, so I held her or carried her all the time. It surprised me when she started clinging to Ron. Even before Sarah was born, he became one of the few people Natalie would go to, and the only person who could get her to sleep.

Later on, after having my wisdom teeth pulled, my mom was watching Natalie and she called me up late one night: "How do you get this baby to sleep?" she begged. And I said, "I call Ron." So mom called Ron. He came over, walked her around the park, and she fell asleep on his shoulder. He was a comfort to her then, and always has been.

It wasn't long before Ron asked me to marry him, but I told him straight up, "Ron, I don't think I love you like that. You're my friend. You're like a brother."

"I messed it up the first time," I told him, "and I am not messing this up again. I am not going to marry you or anyone in a hurry, or at least until I am sure."

I wanted to have all the butterflies. I wanted to know that the love would last, and I wanted to marry for all the right reasons. But I expected to have the fireworks going off in my brain. "I'm waiting for all those signs," I said, "and I'm not doing anything until I get all those signs."

The reality is, I was scared to death. I didn't even know how to tell him that, because I wasn't yet able to trust anyone.

Ron didn't let my hesitation get in the way. He kept showing up. If I called him for anything, he would be there within half an hour. No matter what he was doing, he would drop it and come.

God must've been reading my journals, because Ron was clearly my second chance.

No matter what we did, we had so much fun together. He loved that we were already like a family. After a really good day, we would get into these back-and-forth talks about marriage, and he'd say, "I'd be a really good husband to you, Jenny. I'd always be good to you, I promise."

By this time he knew all about what had happened in my first marriage, and he had witnessed some abuse in his own home growing up. So he made a solemn promise to never be that way. Ever.

"I believe you," I said, "but I have to get an answer"—meaning an answer from God.

When a sign didn't come, Ron finally said to me, "I think you should pray for an answer."

"I *have* been praying for an answer," I said.

"Then maybe you need to pray for a *specific* answer," he responded.

"Okay," I said. "I'll pray harder."

Every night for the next week, I prayed: "Heavenly Father, I need an answer. I don't want to make a mistake again. I'm here and I'm confused, and I need your help. I need a sign that tells me he's the one I should marry."

I prayed about it in the morning, and I prayed about it in the car. I prayed at night when I rocked Natalie and Sarah to sleep, and I prayed on it on Sundays at church.

I went to my mom that week and I said, "Mom, I don't want to make a mistake. I don't want to do the wrong thing again. I don't ever want to put myself or you guys through that again. I want to do this right."

My mom stopped what she was doing and looked me in the eyes and said, "Oh, Jenny, that I could've chosen as well as Ron."

I was stunned!

And that night, I had a dream.

I'm generally not much of a dreamer, but in this dream I walked into the old-fashioned soda shop in Spreckels, where we would go to buy our candy when we were kids. The soda fountain was on the left-hand side, and there were five stools in front of the counter. There were men sitting on those stools. And I might have been half asleep, because I remember thinking, *Why am I having this dream?*

The first guy turned to me and said, "Hey, you should marry me because I'll be a really good father to your children." And I thought, *Oh, okay, that might be good. I'll think about that.* Then I walked in a little further and the next guy said, "Hey, you should marry *me* because I'll be a really good husband to you." And then the next guy said, "You should marry me because I'll work hard to support you, financially."

One after the other they stopped me, and each one told me why I should marry him.

When I got to the end of the counter, I was so confused. I thought, *Now what do I do? I have all these options and I only wanted to know about* one *option.* That's when I noticed another man beside me, and he took my shoulders and turned me around, and said, "Look."

I looked back at the five men sitting at the counter—and they were all Ron. Every one of them was Ron. And in that instant I knew. I had my answer. Ron could give me everything.

The next day I woke up and went to talk to Ron. I said, "All right, here's the deal. I had a dream. I think you'd be a really good husband. You're already a good father to these little girls I have. They love you. You're the only one that can put Natalie to sleep, you know? But I don't think I love you like that. I still don't have those kinds of feelings. I do love you, like a friend. But I think maybe I am supposed to marry you, so is that enough?"

And right there, right then, Ron knelt down in front of me and he took both of my hands in his and he said, "Jenny, I will love you so much that you will learn how to love me."

**RON HAD ALWAYS** loved me so much. And I'm telling you, the minute you give your heart over to a love like that, you feel it. Once I did, those feelings came so fast.

After all the signs that had been there along the way, I'm not sure why I needed to experience the brick-in-the-head moment of that dream. My guess is that I'm just a brick-in-the-head kind of learner.

But here's what I know now: if I hadn't had a marriage go so bad, I don't think I would have chosen a man like Ron.

Had I not been through everything I went through with my first husband, I might not have appreciated the value of Ron's love.

I always try to remember that whenever I'm going through anything that seems too difficult to go through at the time.

As Ron likes to put it, "We never know why God gives us a refining fire. We don't know what he might be refining us for."

5

# Bacon Fights
# & Baby Makes Four

*April 7, 1980*

*Tonight I cut out my wedding dress. You know I've sewn a million things, and I was scared to death to cut this one out. So I went over to Mrs. Wheatley's house, and she helped me. She really is good to me, like a second mom. My dress should be beautiful. It will be an empire styling with buttons up the neck, straight sleeves, and the neatest part will be the lace cape. It will hang elbow length in front and bottom length in back. It should be terrific. Easter just ended, and I had Darrell all week. [Darrell is my sister's boy.] It was an interesting experience. I have so much compassion for him. I just hope he will be all right through all his parents' trials. I hope he knows he can come to me any time. I will be married in less than 11 days. Isn't that exciting? I love Ron so much, and I am looking*

*forward to being a full-fledged family. This is a quip from Natalie.*
*I was scolding her for something, and I called her by name, and she*
*said, "Don't call me that. Dad calls me Princess. You must call me*
*Princess. And we call him Honey. Huh, Mom?" It was so cute. "And*
*we call him Honey."*

———

Ron and I paid for most of our wedding expenses ourselves. I wasn't working full-time, but I did make a little bit of income doing alterations and repairs for the local YMCA, mending T-shirts, and gym shorts, and jockstraps (oh my!). I've sewn together more jockstraps than a woman should ever have to look at in her life!

But times were tight. As I mentioned in my journal, I made my own dress with the help of my friend's mother. I had made a lot of clothing by the time I was twenty-three, but this was a *wedding dress*. Having the help of a talented seamstress really took away my fear. What I wanted was a simple, long-sleeve, white satin dress with an empire waist, and I quickly learned from her that a wedding dress is the same as a regular dress. It's just made of white fabric. It's still sleeves and a zipper, a few buttons and a pleat. I mean, it's basically the same thing you put in everything else. I really shouldn't have been intimidated at all. Adding a lace capelet to come over the front was my idea, and I made that part all by myself.

I also got my own flowers, and because I'm a good hippie, I wore baby's breath and little daisy flowers in my hair.

My sisters didn't go the homemade route. They all wore nice dresses from the Gunne Sax outlet up in San Francisco, which were all the rage at the time. Those dresses had puffy sleeves, all lacy and flowy, but not satiny or silky, more cottony.

Ron's sister was planning to make the wedding cake from scratch, but she got nervous and ordered one from Albertson's grocery store instead. It wasn't perfect, but it was a carrot cake, which I love.

The wedding itself was held at the nearest temple, up in Oakland. Ron was so nervous he left the wedding license at home, and someone had to drive it up. Then he forgot the rings in a locker where he got dressed downstairs. He had to run down and get them right before the ceremony began. But once I came in and he saw me in my dress, once we held each other's hands and looked into each other's eyes, all the nerves melted away.

I could hardly remember why I'd been hesitant about this marriage at all.

Our ceremony was in the morning, followed by a luncheon at Ron's parents' house, followed by a reception that evening back at my parents' house in Spreckels. Nearly a hundred people came through those little rooms in my parents' Victorian to wish us well. Our families mixed pretty well, even though I later learned that Ron's parents were not too excited about our marriage in the beginning. Turns out they were worried that I was some "heathen" divorced woman! But once they got to know me better, it all worked out.

It was Ron's dream to stay in a hotel room with a fireplace, so the two of us spent our wedding night being warmed by a fire at a little hotel over in Monterey. Then we woke up and hopped in my dad's Mazda to make the drive to Bear Lake, Idaho.

I'm not sure why we bought a honeymoon package in Bear Lake, other than somebody said it was their favorite place. We looked it up and saw they had a honeymoon package for a rock-bottom price. But we drove about fourteen hours, through Nevada and Utah and all the way into Idaho, and when we got there, there were two cars in the whole parking lot. The resort was huge, with lakes and pools and tennis courts. But it was April, so everything was still frozen.

"Can we just have our money back?" I asked.

They said yes, which I thought was very nice, and we decided to make the best of it by taking a long, slow road-trip back home.

That's when we noticed a hotel with a neon "Waterbeds" sign.

"Oh! Let's stay there!" I said.

"What? What for?" Ron asked.

"I've never slept in a waterbed. Have you?"

"No," he said.

"Well, let's try it! Let's go to a different hotel every night and try all the different kinds of beds!"

Ron just laughed and said, "Okay!"

He has always been supportive of my ideas—even the crazy ones!

Well, we checked in and went to the room and sat down on the edge of the waterbed, and our backsides hit the board. When one of us moved, the other one would fall over! We just laughed and laughed, and neither of us got much sleep that night. We learned pretty quickly that hotels with waterbeds are *not* four-star hotels.

Driving through Idaho and Utah in the springtime, we spotted all these beautiful waterfalls that just randomly came down the mountains by the side of the road. We stopped and took pictures of every one of them.

We've never been able to find all the photographs we took during that trip. We lost them.

But we pieced together a honeymoon from the scrapped plans we'd made, and we loved every minute of it.

After we were married, I said to Ron, "We've already got these two little kids, so if you want to have a couple more kids, let's just go ahead and have them."

My mom had her last baby when she was forty, and that seemed really late to me, so I was determined to have my family done by the time I was thirty. It didn't matter to me if I had two kids or ten kids. I knew I wanted to have them when I was young.

A couple of months after the wedding, I started throwing up all the time. It felt like a really bad stomach flu. A part of me knew that I might be pregnant, because, well, we had tried out all those beds! But I had never been so sick with my other pregnancies.

Sure enough, the doctor said, "You're pregnant!"

"All right, then," I said.

That night, I waited a bit to tell Ron. I waited until we were at a restaurant, and then I blurted it out as soon as we sat down: "Ron, I'm pregnant."

His face lit up like a Christmas tree.

"Really?" he said with the biggest smile I'd ever seen on him.

"Yup. Really."

He was so excited that he got up and came over to my side of the table and hugged me, and kissed me, with tears in his eyes.

You can bet I cried too. Some of the happiest tears ever.

RON DECIDED PRETTY QUICKLY THAT we needed to live in a house that was bigger than the tiny duplex we shared, so he went out and found a rental in nearby Salinas. It would be the first of many moves we'd make in the next few years.

As the weeks went on, I was sicker than I'd ever been. I'd barely leave the toilet with enough time to change a diaper before I'd be back at it again.

I kept wondering, *How could feeling this sick* possibly *be normal?* But the doctor insisted it was.

I guess *normal* doesn't always mean *comfortable.*

Maybe that applies to marriage too.

On our first Christmas morning as a married couple, Ron's big present to me was a toolbox with my name engraved on it.

I called my mother, bawling: "Mom, he gave me a *toolbox.*"

And she said, "Jenny, for a mechanic, that is probably the most personal thing he could give you."

**RON:** She loved working on houses. I thought it was a nice gift!

Like any young couple, we occasionally fought. It happened rarely, let me tell you, because it takes two people to fight and Ron is *not* a fighter. But when we did argue in the beginning, it was rough.

One time I called my mom and said, "Is it normal for couples to fight?" And she said, "Oh, yeah, that's very normal."

But she went on to share something personal and important with me: "One day, I was mad at your dad all day long, and by the afternoon, I was furious. Then I stopped and tried to remember what I was actually mad about. And I thought about it and thought about it, and I remembered it started because he had insulted the way I cook bacon. That's when I decided that I didn't want to let bacon ruin my marriage, or to make me so angry with him that I carried it around all day long."

After that call, whenever I would get angry at Ron, I would think about that—because so much of what we're angry about doesn't matter. It just doesn't. I had to figure out what mattered and when. Some big things do matter, but what we usually get insulted about or angry about, it's the little stuff. Seriously, are we going to ruin our relationships over bacon? Or the laundry? I think a lot of people give way too much credence to these little things, and they walk around with hurt feelings being mad about stuff. I didn't want to do that. And for my part, I figured it was my job to use the gifts that I was given to contribute, and to create, and to help this family. So I tried really hard.

Still, in those early days, I would go back to my mother's house a lot, where I knew the girls would get all kinds of affection and I wouldn't be the only one cooking and cleaning for them while Ron was at work.

My mother loved on those grandkids. So did my dad. But one day my mother said to me, "Jenny, you need to go home and take care of your family and stop coming here every single day."

I was shocked and hurt. But then I realized she was right.

In order to find my real joy in raising kids as a stay-at-home mom, I had to flip a switch and recognize that this was *my* job. Not somebody else's. Mine.

Flipping the switch for me meant accepting: "I am the mom. I am the wife." It wasn't right for me to put that work onto my mother quite as often as I was. But I also knew there had to be more to raising kids than just work. So I decided that if I was going to give this my all, I was going to have a whole lot of fun while I did it.

As if my pregnancy-sickness and the daily exhaustion of raising two babies under two weren't enough of a challenge, Ron and I decided to add another child to our growing family even before the new baby was born.

My sister's son, Darrell, was then seven years old.

Darrell had spent a lot of time living at my mom and dad's house while my sister did her best to sort out her life, and he had stayed with me on-and-off after I got my little duplex too. He was used to playing with Natalie, and he loved Sarah, and they all got along so well.

With my parents getting older, and with Ron and me having some more room in the new house, we decided to see if Darrell wanted to move in with us full-time. And he did.

Some people might think throwing a third kid into the mix would be more than a new mom could take, but I didn't feel that way. Darrell was so good to have around. He kept Natalie and Sarah both entertained, and we loved having an older child to care for. So a few months into our marriage, Ron became Dad to three kids that weren't his. And he loved it! He loved being a dad so much that we went ahead and filed paperwork so he could adopt Natalie and Sarah and make our family even more official than it already was. (I think he would've gladly adopted Darrell, too, but it was a little soon for that.)

Through all the nausea and feedings and diapers and adjustments to life with three kids, Ron never complained. He was just so happy to be with me, and to have a family, which made me so happy to be with him.

Was our home life perfect? No! Ron and I had to learn to work together on more than a few things. And no doubt it was harder than it might have been because I was still carrying some baggage from my first marriage. I had some real obstacles from that. Mostly I needed to learn how to trust again in order to get back to being myself.

Being with a loving man who loved my kids made a powerful difference.

———

About a year into our marriage, my ex-husband called me up and said, "Hey, did you get the papers? You know, the ones I had to sign because your new husband wants to adopt the children so bad?"

"No," I said. "I didn't."

"Good," he said. "I changed my mind."

It wasn't the first time he had done this, and in the past it really got to me. On those previous calls, I got off the phone with him and broke down and cried.

Not this time.

My ex started talking about how he'd never allow the adoption to happen, and I stopped him right there.

"Okay," I said. "I've decided not to worry about it."

"What do you mean?" he said. "Why not?"

"Because if you don't send those papers, then I want you to send all the money that you owe me in child support."

"You said you'd never do that," he said.

"Well, guess what?" I said. "*I changed my mind.*"

I hung up on him and Ron whirled around in the kitchen and looked at me so fast and said, "Now *that's* the girl I remember!"


BEFORE WE KNEW IT, THE signed paperwork appeared in our mailbox and Ron officially became Natalie's and Sarah's adopted dad—just in time for our first baby together, our fourth child, to join the family.

My first two babies were born in hospitals, and I didn't love the hospital experience. This time, I wanted the birth experience to be as natural as possible. Thankfully, I wasn't the only one: the idea of having a "natural birth" was gaining popularity at the time.

Ron agreed that I should do things just how I wanted. So, even though our insurance wouldn't cover it, we hired midwives and made plans to have our baby at home.

I did a lot of research into the birthing process, thinking that I might want to be a midwife myself one day. And I found myself leaning toward the Leboyer method, where you actually give birth in water. I couldn't do it myself because we didn't have a hot tub at home, or even a bathtub big enough. So I improvised.

When I felt that our baby was about to be born, we called the midwives and I had Ron fill our little red Coleman ice chest with warm water. We placed it right next to the bed. But the midwives took one look at me and said this baby wouldn't come for hours. "Go take a walk," they said. So I did. I walked around the block and came right back and said, "I'm pretty sure I'm gonna have this baby really soon!"

They all sort of looked at me and shook their heads, but one of them said, "Let me check you with this next contraction." So I got on the couch and she checked me, and her eyes got real wide, and she said, "Where do you want to have this baby?"

"In my bedroom," I said.

"Then go. Go *now!*" she told me.

We hurried to the bedroom, and Ron was right there, and I got one leg up on the bed, and Hillary was born right that moment! One of the midwives fell to her knees and caught her as Ron looked on in shock with his mouth wide open. "Do they all happen like this?" he asked.

"No," the midwife chuckled. "This is very unusual. *Very* unusual."

As she handed me our little girl, I could hardly believe how much hair she had. My other babies were born bald, with very little hair. She had hair on her ears, hair on her shoulders. If I hadn't seen her come out of my own body, I would've thought they switched babies on me. Seriously.

Almost immediately she started crying the most stressful, worried little sound, and I noticed she had worn a little suck mark on her arm. Her tiny body was all tensed up.

But we put our little Hillary down in that tub of warm water, and her arms gently floated out to the side. She stopped crying. She relaxed. Her eyes came open and Ron and I just held her right there.

She looked so peaceful—floating in our red Coleman ice chest.

**WE DIDN'T KNOW** this when we first moved in, but there was a lot of gang stuff going on in the neighborhood where Hillary was born. We were pretty scared about it when we figured it out. Especially when we learned that one of the heads of the gangs happened to be our next-door neighbor. But those fears didn't last very long.

What I learned pretty quickly is that they were all just like the rest of us. They were all just trying to find a place to belong. So we were kind to them. We brought them cookies, the same way we did for our neighbors wherever we moved. And they appreciated that.

One day, somebody pulled up on the road. And then a bunch of cars pulled up right after. I went outside and our neighbor came over and said, "You need to go inside. Get your kids. Take them inside. This don't involve you. Just stay inside."

Because we were friendly, they were protective of us. And we were so grateful.

A little kindness went a long way.

It usually does.

# People Pears, Prayers & Possibilities

I was never one of those women who felt like, *Oh my gosh, what am I gonna do with all these kids?* I loved it. All of it. When people think about, *What do you want to be when you grow up,* all I ever really wanted to be was a mom. And I felt like what I was doing was crucial and important. Every single day mattered.

But with Darrell turning nine, Natalie four, Sarah three, Hillary growing fast, and—surprise!—another baby on the way, we needed more space. So we moved to another rental house in a different area of Salinas.

We were lucky to find a big enough place that we could afford. We didn't have a lot of options. Ron had a good job as a machinist, but with such a big family, it was tough to make ends meet.

We came to rely on the kindness of neighbors, friends, church members, and even strangers, more than I ever could have imagined.

People just seemed to know we were struggling. When your husband works at a factory, I suppose you can't have a big family without people knowing that you're struggling. And so, we were always getting a call: "Oh, I have extra tomatoes. Do you want them?" I never turned food down. I couldn't afford to. I would can it, I would cook it up, I would freeze it. I was so grateful for all these blessings that were coming our way, and part of being grateful to me meant that I didn't waste it. Somebody had given it to us. If I didn't make time to can those peaches, they would go bad. So I made time to can those peaches!

One time, Ron's brother came over when we were canning pears and I said, "If you come into my kitchen and I'm canning, you'd better pick up a knife." So he picked up a knife, and when he was done peeling he had carved faces in all of them. That whole season we had these jars of pears that were like little people looking out of the pantry. The kids thought it was hilarious. Every time we looked at those people-pears we couldn't help but laugh and think of Uncle Dennis.

Even as we struggled, and in fact *especially* as we struggled, we gave money to our church to help others. We paid tithing, like a lot of people do at a lot of different churches. And I can say in all honesty that as long as we paid tithing, whatever happened, whatever situation we were in, we had enough. If we were down to our last penny, somebody would call. We were able to make it. And, oddly enough, whenever we got behind in our tithing, certain things seemed to get worse. So, while other people might look at it as strange to be giving when you have so little, I counted it as one of our many blessings.

As it says in scripture:

If you pay your tithes the Lord will open up the windows of heaven and pour you out a blessing that there shall not be room enough to receive it. Malachi 3:10

How blessed were we to be together, with a roof over our heads, with four healthy children and a fifth on the way? And to get to experience the joy of how different and unique each child can turn out to be?

Even as youngsters, the differences were so clear. Natalie was a little mother. She always wanted to help me. And I already mentioned that she was a snuggly child.

Well, Sarah wasn't a cuddler like her sister. She wanted her bottle propped, and she didn't want to be held close and tight. She was just easygoing. Whatever came up, she was a happy little kid.

And then Hillary came along, and as soon as she learned to walk she turned into the child who would shyly hide behind my leg whenever we went somewhere and met someone new. She was always in a world of imagination. She was our watcher, our learner—one of those children you gave a little talent to and they made it bigger.

There were times when I was in that house, pregnant, trying to cook dinner as I tended to Hillary while Natalie and Darrell were playing together, when Sarah and Ron would go sit together outside on the steps of the front porch. They would listen to the sound of the birds, and the music spilling out from the rolled-down windows of passing cars. I could hear their conversation through the screen door as Ron would say, "Do you hear that engine? What is it? Yamaha, Honda, or Harley-Davidson?" It wasn't long before Sarah could recognize the sounds of those bike engines and name them before they came around the corner, and the two of them would giggle every time she did it.

Their conversation was the sweetest sound to my ears.

When Alan was born, in 1982, it was in a birthing room at the hospital, which was so much more comfortable than the old hospital rooms. But when I asked the nurses to please take the bedding out and fill the plastic bassinet with warm water, so we could place Alan in it right after he was born, they wouldn't allow it. Hillary was the only one of my babies who got to enjoy a post-birth baby bath.

We were in there quite a while. My back was killing me. I was laboring, I was standing, I was sitting, I kept lying down, and nothing helped. So we turned on the TV and started watching *A Star is Born*, with Barbra Streisand, and right in the middle of it I said to Ron, "It's time." Alan arrived shortly after that, and to this day we still laugh about that movie.

As Alan fell asleep on my chest in the quiet of that birthing room, which felt more like a nice hotel room, I looked at the nurse and whispered, "How long can I stay here?"

"You can go home after six hours," the nurse said.

I re-asked the question: "No, no, no. I'm not asking when I can *go home*. I'm asking how long can I *stay here*?"

I had four kids at home. I needed the break!

To HIS DETRIMENT AND HIS joy, Alan was treated like the little prince in our family. Ron and I tried to treat every child the same way, but the girls and even Darrell doted over our little baby boy.

*Little* is the wrong word. As a baby, Alan grew an inch and a pound a week. We went to the doctor and said, "This can't be normal." But the doctor, a small Italian man, looked up at Ron and me who just towered over him, and said, "Well, you're not gonna have *little* children."

Alan was so tall that he was the kid who kept everybody saying, "I can't believe he's still doing that," whether it was crawling, or sitting in a high chair. And I'd have to answer for him, "He's only two!" He just kept growing. His shoe size was whatever age he was. From the time he was ten he wore size 10, then he wore an 11, a 12, and so on up to size 17.

Alan believed he could do anything. When Alan was only three or four, Ron got him a sixteen-inch bike with training wheels. He rode it a lot and one day he broke the trainers, but instead of waiting for us to fix them or put on some new ones, Ron sat him back on it and Alan took off on two wheels.

Ron says Alan takes after me that way: "He just figures things out."

I'm not sure why I've always had that knack, but it sure came in handy with five kids—'cause there was a lot we needed to figure out!

Thank goodness for Ron. Whenever he was home, he took over and let me rest as much as he could. And as our family kept growing, I can't remember him complaining, "We can't afford this," or "We can't handle this." He had fun with it, like I did.

Right after Alan was born, Ron took the rest of the kids out for some fast-food drive-thru before they came to see us at the hospital, and they came in with stains all over their clothes. Everything was red and yellow splotches. It looked like they'd been in a food fight.

I said, "Ron! Don't you know the food rules?"

"The food rules?" he said.

"Yes! If you dress your child in a white shirt, they can only eat French fries and 7-Up. You cannot give them ketchup, you cannot give them Hi-C! If they're wearing red, they can have the fruit punch and ketchup. It's fine."

"I didn't know there were food rules," he said.

I laughed. It really was funny. I was joking, as I often was, but from that day forward Ron tried to match the color of the food he gave 'em to the colors of the kids' outfits.

Laundry got a whole lot easier after that.

Bath time got more complicated, though.

There's a funny Shel Silverstein poem that says, "There's too many kids in this tub . . . I just washed a behind that I'm sure wasn't mine." It has stanza after stanza of all these funny things, and I would often read that poem to my kids. And the funniest thing to me was I had these three darling girls, sitting in the bathtub acting like darling little girls do as they played in the water, and the moment I put Alan in at six or seven months, as soon as he could sit up on his own, he went *"Ruff. Rum. Splash. Splash."* And the girls started screaming like there was a monster in the tub.

I hadn't taught Alan any different. The only example he had to follow was theirs. But he was his own unique character.

I loved that.

I loved how different every child in our family was.

———

A few months after Alan was born, we found out the owners of the house we were renting had sold it.

We had to move, and we had to move quickly.

We knew that finding a house that could hold five children on our limited budget would not be easy. But we kept reminding each other: "We're never gonna let them starve, and they don't have to drive the nicest car or wear the fanciest clothing. These kids will be loved, and that's all that matters."

Still, I prayed and prayed: "Heavenly Father, we need another house, and it really needs to be bigger than the one we have now, and we have to be able to afford it. I know you know all these things, but I just wanna let you know that we need a bigger house, and we need it fast!"

Within a week of that prayer, a member of our church came to us and said, "So, there's this huge house out on Blanco Road, and they've decided to rent it out. Nobody's lived in it for a long time. It needs a lot of repair, but nobody's living in it now. We thought of your family right away. They only want $200 a month for it."

Driving up, it looked like a mansion—this big stately farm-house in the middle of acres of fields, surrounded by rose gardens and eucalyptus trees. Once we got a little closer, we could see the disrepair. The rose gardens were mostly weed-and-thorn gardens. The shutters were hanging off. The faucets were rusted and hadn't been turned on in decades. The plaster walls were cracked and falling apart. The floors were broken and heaved where water had gotten in. I think most people would've turned around and said, "There's no way we can move our family into that mess."

Not me and Ron. We said, "Oh my goodness. Yes. We'll take it!"

All we saw were the possibilities. I fell in love with it, and I was so grateful. It had a porch that wrapped all the way around the outside. Almost all of the inside wood was eucalyptus imported from Australia. That wood was so hard, they had to have everything drilled and pegged. And it had two staircases: a double-wide staircase in the front of the house that looked like something a bride would walk down, and a back staircase that wasn't really a staircase at all. It was a carpeted ramp that went from the top-to-bottom of the house, which was originally built for servants to push carts up and down.

With seven bedrooms upstairs, we were able to choose a nursery close to our bedroom, and then each of our kids could take their pick. At the end of the second night, though, they were all together again in two rooms.

They didn't want to sleep apart.

They had never slept apart, and they didn't want to sleep apart now.

7

# Unexpected Blessings

When Darrell was about to turn eleven, Ron and I realized that he'd been living either with my parents or with us, off and on (mostly on), for the better part of a decade. So we started talking about adopting him. He was as much a part of our family as any of our kids, so adoption just made sense to us. It would take us a couple of years before we could make it official, but we were sure it was the right thing to do.

Thankfully, I wasn't alone trying to figure all of this wife and mother stuff out. I had friends, and we had a weekly women's meeting at church on Sundays, where we would talk about all sorts of topics, from bedtimes, to chores, to teaching kids right from wrong, and making sure we made time for ourselves and our husbands too. And if there's one thing I learned it's that when you're raising kids, it's okay to say no to things that pull you away from your family and might wear you out.

I also learned that it's okay to say yes to self-care.

When Ron came home at five o'clock most days, I would say to him, "I need half an hour." I would go sit in the bedroom and turn on the TV, and the only thing on that time of day on the channels we got with our antenna was *The Streets of San Francisco*. So I watched while he took over, and then came back out refreshed and ready to take on the work of the night.

That half hour made all the difference in the world.

I wrote the word *NO* in big letters and taped it up on the wall by my phone, to remind myself that heeding calls to go help with a theater program or even to see friends sometimes was too much for me. Then I realized it wasn't always polite to just say no, so I changed the sign to say, "Let me think about it; I'll call you later."

I didn't stop doing *everything*. But with five kids, I had to pick and choose more carefully.

Because I could sew, I could decorate, and a lot of things came naturally to me, people asked me to do a lot. For example, we had about eighty children ages three to twelve in the families at our church, and I served as president of that age group. Which meant I was responsible for getting all the teachers for the children, and I was responsible for putting together events, which took a lot of time and effort. But that work also involved my own children and brought me some relief, because there were other adults that I interacted with, and it kept my kids entertained and gave them things to do. So that was a good use of my time and energy, which was stretched so thin.

Plus, it was a form of giving back, and I *wanted* to give back—because there were times when we couldn't have done any of what we were doing without our church. Our church has its own welfare program. It's a wonderful program that helps feed millions of people all over the world. And they have a whole industry side, where if, for example, you needed a table, you could help assemble that table, or work doing other things so they would be able to give that table to you or to whomever needed it. There were only a couple of times when we needed the help, because we tried really hard to be self-sufficient and resourceful. But in those times, our church community meant everything to us.

All of that was worth more than a little bit of my time and effort outside the home, because it was generous, and it served a purpose.

So were my trips to the Daily Bread Stores.

We had Daily Bread Stores in our area that sold products that were past their expiration date. And I would drive around to the Daily Bread Stores when they were getting rid of the day-old stuff that was already *days* old, and I would take that to families like my own who needed it. My kids helped with that, and saw the smiles, and experienced the gratitude when we visited those families. Plus they got to eat all sorts of Hostess Twinkies and Pies. (They may have been a week or more beyond the "best by" date, but they were still delicious.)

On days when we couldn't make it, we had a friend with a pig farm who would go pick up the Daily Bread Store throwaway stuff too, for his pigs, but before he took it home he'd stop by our house and ask, "You guys want any of this?" We would take what we could use and combine it with whatever we could find at the crash-and-dent stores. That's where they sold dented canned food at bargain-basement prices. A place where two dollars went really far. We would piece whatever we got all together and turn it into meals.

We had no choice but to be resourceful, and it turned out that I was really good at that.

One of our favorite games became piecing things together in the kitchen: "I have this, this, and this. What can I make?" It was a fun way to deal with the fact that we were often in a place of, "All right, we've got rice. We've got canned tomatoes. What can we do?"

––––––––

Everything was working out pretty good for us, for the most part, right up until the summer of 1984.

For some reason, after our next child, Jacob, was born that July, I went into a really severe case of after-baby-blues. I grew so sad, and anxious, and scared—I could have crawled into that little place behind the toilet and hid back there. I couldn't even go out of my house. I was just having such a hard time, and I didn't know what was happening to me. This had never happened to me before.

Thankfully there was a woman from church who came to check on me regularly. I didn't know her very well, but I call her a dear friend now because she showed up. I mean truly showed up. She never called. If she had called, I would have told her not to come. I would have told her, "I'm fine. Thanks, but no thanks." Instead, she showed up with her two kids in the car and said things like, "Hey, we're going to the beach today. Can I take your kids along?"

It was such a relief for me.

I don't know if I ever told her how deeply grateful I was to her for doing that.

I don't even remember a lot of what happened, but I do remember Ron taking my car keys away from me. If I got in the car, he said, he was afraid I wouldn't stop at a stoplight because I was too afraid somebody would see me. My anxiety was *that* high.

Ron started coming home from work in the middle of the day to feed Jacob, because I couldn't bring myself to feed him. He would come home and make sure all the kids had lunch. He was just a champion.

He was my saving grace. He was what I couldn't be.

On a day when I was more down than ever, I decided to go talk to my mom about it. I took the keys and I drove over to see her, but she had somebody in her little bookstore at the front of her house. So, rather than risk being seen, I snuck in the back door, up the stairs, and hid in my brother's room.

My mother saw my car outside and she thought she had heard the back door close, so after her customer left, she called out, "Jenny? Jenny?"

She climbed the stairs and found me curled up and hiding in a corner.

"Jenny," she said, "you need to go to the doctor."

"I can't," I said. "I *can't* go to the doctor."

She finally talked me through it and drove me to the doctor herself.

It was terrifying for me because I'd always been the easygoing one; I'd always been the "nothing bothers me" one. I didn't know how to fix this.

**RON:** She was really changed. It was scary. I kept explaining to everybody, "She never does this. This is something new. She never does this." And the thing I'm grateful for is that once she recognized just how bad it was, Jenny accepted some help. She wanted to find the best doctor. She let us help her.

Somebody said to me during that time, "Well, if you didn't have so many children . . ." and the mother bear in me roared up. I cut them off. I think it would have hurt less if they had slapped me across the face. I said, "If I didn't have this many children, I would have jumped outta the window a long time ago. It's because of these children that I actually get up and try."

I knew these little people needed me—Darrel, Natalie, Sarah, Hillary, Alan, and now Jacob.

I was someone who never wanted to go on medication. But this was too much. The doctor gave me a prescription, and it helped. I was so thankful. I got back to being "me."

Eventually, I was able to go off the medication, and when I did, I realized what a gift Jake had given me. Once I came through it, I realized that going through postpartum depression was one of the most powerful things that had ever happened to me—because it gave me *empathy*.

I'm not proud of this, but up until then I think I quietly carried a lot of judgment around with me. I wasn't even aware of it, but when I saw other people struggling with their mental health, I sometimes thought, *Well, you should just be stronger,* or, *You should just do this or do that and figure it out.* But I learned that it doesn't have anything to do with what a person is "choosing" to do. When I was dealing with things like anxiety and depression, I realized a person has no control over that. I needed help. And thankfully, I got help.

My experience gave me so much empathy for my sister and her challenges, and for other people who go through these types of things.

I have been grateful for that lesson ever since.

---

A fter two years and a whole lot of hard work, that old mansion-like house we were renting was starting to look pretty good. That's when the owners unexpectedly decided that they didn't want to rent it to our family anymore. Which meant that we had to move. Again.

Can you imagine the looks you get when you tell a potential landlord that you have six children. "And did I mention that we have another on the way?" I was pregnant again. We searched and searched for something that would fit us all and wouldn't cost a fortune, and in the end a friend from Ron's work found a solution. He offered to rent us a house that happened to be divided up into four small bedrooms. The rent was $700 a month—$500 more than we were currently paying for a much bigger house.

Given everything else we'd seen, we knew it was the best we could do. So we took it, gratefully. We never let the kids get down about the move. Not for one second. "Wait 'til you see it!" we told them. We made everything fun. We got them excited about the idea of having bunk beds, and figuring out who would get the top bunk. We talked about how much fun it would be to have a boys' room and a girls' room, and how important it was for Darrell to have his own room, because he was the oldest—and that they could get their own room when they were the oldest too. We also talked up how nice it would be to be in a neighborhood instead of out in the fields.

Of course, moving is one of the most stressful and difficult things a family can do. And we made the move just a week before our next child, Josh, was born, in December of 1985. I won't sugarcoat it: I hurt. I collapsed on the bed at the end of each day, after moving and juggling everything, just completely exhausted. I looked at the gold-flocked wallpaper in this home, which they didn't want us to change or remodel in any way, and I cried.

Ron was amazing, though. One night, he brought home some Oreo cookies and a jug of milk. Not the no-name, copycat Oreos. I'm talking about the real thing. And not the powdered milk that we drank in our family, either, but a half-gallon of real, whole milk that we never could have afforded as part of our regular weekly food budget. The two of us snuck into our bedroom and locked the door and ate and drank every bit of that treat, and *oh* did it make us smile! It was such a splurge.

If we didn't make the best of things, we would've made ourselves miserable. So we chose to make the best of things. Always.

No matter how down I got at times in that house, I would wake up the next morning to the giggles and shenanigans of those children and I couldn't help but smile. I'd give my worries to God, and the fun would start all over again.

And at night, as we got the kids settled down for bed, I always asked them, "What was the best part of your day?"

"Getting an A on my test!" "Eating cupcakes!" "Singing!"

It didn't matter what good thing they remembered. All that mattered to me is that each of my children went to bed thinking about something good.

------

About a year after Josh was born, the kids decided they wanted to go to Disneyland. There was no way we could afford the entrance for nine people. We couldn't even afford to go to the movies with such a large family. But I didn't want to let them down.

"We can go," I told them, "but you'll have to earn your admission."

This was before Christmas, and while we didn't have much, we did have a friend in California who had a ranch with mistletoe growing on it. So we got an idea. The children got permission and we went over and picked some. They put it into baggies, and we tied red bows or ribbons on every single one. Then they got all dressed up in matching sweatshirts with Christmas trees on them, which I made for them, and they filled up a wagon with mistletoe. Sarah and Hillary pulled the wagon all around the neighborhood as Alan and Natalie went door-to-door to offer the sale. Jake handed it out, and little Josh just went along for the ride, smiling at the customers from the wagon. They sold the whole wagonload and put every single dollar, quarter, nickel, dime, and penny into a big gallon-size pickle jar in the kitchen.

I knew that if I had cashed that change in, it wouldn't have meant the same to them, so we watched that pickle jar fill up little by little for days, and then weeks.

When their efforts at mistletoe sales weren't enough, they put their minds into figuring it out. That's when one of the kids came up with the idea to sell candy bars. We talked it over with Ron. He agreed we could front the initial cost from our grocery money and off to Costco we went to buy some bulk boxes for the cheapest price around. The candy bars cost twenty-five cents each, and they had to reimburse that part, but they would make seventy-five cents for each sale if they sold them for one dollar. In those days, a lot of kids were going door-to-door selling candy bars for their school sports team or their after-school clubs. My kids? When someone asked if they were selling them for their group or team they said, "No, we're just trying to get to Disneyland."

I knew we would need to pack a lot of food for the trip, so for my part I started storing it up. Whenever I could, I bought an extra box of granola bars and put that aside, or I picked up a box of crackers or cookies at a good sale here and there.

Finally, after many months of saving and selling and working together to earn the entrance tickets, we poured the contents of that giant pickle jar onto the floor, counted it up, and they had done it! We were going to Disneyland! I'm pretty sure their screams of excitement could be heard all the way to the next neighborhood.

When our big day arrived, we loaded up the van and left early in the morning. And maybe forty miles from the Magic Kingdom we stopped at a stoplight and our van died.

Now, to be fair, this was an old van that we bought from a church, and it had quite a few miles on it. There was no head-liner. It had rubber mats covering the rusty spots on the floor, and the bench seats were bolted in. We expected to have some trouble with it from time to time, but it had been working just fine before we left. At first I wasn't too worried because Ron is a good mechanic, so he can usually figure these things out, but after lifting the hood and looking at it for some time, he came back to the window shaking his head. "I don't know," he said softly. "I don't know what it is."

For him to say "I don't know" meant to me that it was proba-bly something big that wasn't going to be cheap to fix.

We were sitting there in the van on the side of the road not moving for quite a while, so all of the kids started getting worried.

They knew the only money we had was sixty-seven dollars, which was just enough for gas to get us to Disney and back. We didn't have extra money for souvenirs, or for the park restaurants, and we certainly didn't plan for towing and repairing the van.

I took a deep breath and did what I always did when I felt lost: I prayed.

I sat straight up and looked ahead (probably because I couldn't bear looking back and seeing their little broken hearts and worried eyes looking at me) and I said to them, "Children. I need you all to pray that this car will run." The car got really, really quiet except for the whisper of their little voices. We sat there, closed our eyes, and prayed together: "Please, God, we really need our van to run."

After a few moments, one little voice broke the quiet and said softly, "Try it, Dad. Just try it."

Ron looked over at me as he put the key into the ignition, and he turned it. And all of a sudden the engine turned over and the van started right up!

Everyone cheered and screamed so loudly you would have thought we won the Super Bowl.

That moment? For me it was another precious example of all the tender mercies, the little blessings of faith, that were given to our family—a family who didn't have a ton but always tried really hard.

And those blessings just filled me up.

———

Three years after moving into that four-bedroom house, we got called into the bishop's office one Sunday after church service.

Usually when you get called into the bishop's office it's because one of your children has done something wrong, or they want to give you a new calling or volunteer position. But that wasn't the case this time at all.

"So, this is some really happy news," the bishop said. "A member of our church has anonymously donated money for your family to have a down payment, so you can buy a house."

We were stunned.

"Wait," I said, "like, *real* money? How *much* money?"

"What they'd like you to do," the bishop said, "is go house shopping and find a house that you like, that will fit your family and that you can afford the payment on, and then we'll let them know what the down payment is—and they'll cover it."

Ron and I looked at each other with tears in our eyes, and for maybe the first time in my life, I was speechless.

8

# Growing Family in the Salad Bowl

W e had to look a little farther inland and south to find a house we could afford, but we found a fixer-upper that suited us just fine. In Greenfield. The broccoli capital of the world.

Greenfield is in the more southern part of the region known as the Salad Bowl. Gilroy, up north, is the garlic capital, and Castroville, closer to the ocean, is the artichoke capital. Our former town, Salinas, is sort of in the middle of those. But Greenfield is much more rural and seemed a million miles away.

It was heavenly.

And the best part? We were in our own home, which meant we could fix it up.

Poor Ron would work all day and then drive the added thirty-minute commute to get back to us and find projects waiting for him. Like the time I took out a big roller and painted on the side of our house "Ron loves Jenny" in giant white letters. The house we bought was pink and I hated the color. Ron took one look at the side of the house and said, "I guess we're painting the house."

I nodded. "Yep. We sure are."

Then I decided we needed to redo the bathroom, so I took the toilet right out and left it in the front room. Ron came home again: "I guess we are redoing the bathroom?"

I nodded. "Yep. We sure are."

And *still*, he rarely complained.

Could I have married a better man?

We did what we could do to fix up the rooms on a tight budget, but we didn't have extra money to furnish all the rooms in that house, so I did what I always did. I prayed. I got down on my knees and I said, "Heavenly Father, we've paid our tithing, and I'm willing to have all the children you want me to have. You can see we are taking care of them and loving them, but we need some help. We need some furniture, and I would like to have a couch." Then, because I love to have fun even in my prayers, I said, "If you'd really like to know, I'd like a navy-blue Italian-leather sectional."

That very afternoon a lady stopped by and said, "Hey, the dentist down the way is selling their couches. I really think you ought to go and look. They might be perfect for your family."

I went right away, because God can open a door but you've got to be ready to walk through it. When I got there, I saw that they weren't blue Italian leather, they were brown Naugahyde, but they were lovely. When I asked about them, they said, "We're changing all of our office furniture." Then they added, "If you want them, you can just have them."

"That would be great. I'll take them!" I said as I laughed with gratitude.

So that very day we had two big couches that fit perfectly in the family room.

But then another lady stopped by and she had two couches in the back of her pickup truck. "We changed the furniture in our house," she said, "and I had a feeling you might like these couches." I smiled. They weren't blue Italian leather either; they were light beige, but I was so thankful. "Yes, *I* do like them. And they would be perfect in our living room. Thank you so much!" I said.

It felt like blessings were pouring down on us like rain.

I walked around the room singing as the kids jumped up and down on the new couches. We could hardly wait for Ron to come home that night, so when we heard his car pull in we all ran outside to meet him with the good news. And that's when I saw that in back of Ron's truck, he had two more couches.

He smiled and said, "Tony's wife came in today and said that she decided to redo her living room and wanted to know if we wanted her couches." They weren't Italian leather, they were blue corduroy, but I couldn't help but laugh.

I shook my head in awe as I looked over at Ron's beaming smile, but I said to him, "Just a minute."

I left him standing there confused in the driveway with the kids as I rushed back into the house, went to the side of our bed, and got down on my knees.

"Heavenly Father," I said, "we thank you for all of the lovely couches. You can stop now."

———

As we settled into the house in Greenfield, we decided to do what many people in California were doing at the time: homeschool the kids. We started with our three girls. Natalie, especially, was having a hard time at school. She had always been super smart, but she was such a perfectionist that she would rip up her papers three times until she got them just right. And the night before exams? She couldn't get any sleep at all. So homeschooling for Natalie was such a blessing. I loved teaching, and I had spent years leading groups and teaching at our church. And I figured as long as the kids knew how to read, they could learn anything.

The school was supportive. They even sent a teacher to come to our house to share the curriculum.

We did everything with a theme. If I was teaching about the ocean, we went to the ocean. We read about the ocean. We checked out books on the ocean. We wrote stories about the ocean. We did math problems related to the ocean. The girls became ocean specialists while splashing around happily in the salty waves and turning over rocks in the afternoon sun.

After a few weeks of witnessing how much fun we were having, the boys grew jealous: "They're having so much fun, we want to come home with them!" Ron and I talked it over and we decided it would be easier and a lot more fun. So I started home-schooling everybody full-time—except for Darrell, who was now sixteen and in high school.

I've already mentioned that every child is different, but it's also worth stating that every *stage* for every child is different too. There are probably few teenage boys who want to stay at home all day with their parents and younger siblings, and being a teenager, Darrell was far less interested in taking instructions from me than he was from his teachers.

We always used to get all the kids' clothing at the thrift store before the start of school because I knew they would grow out of their clothing so fast and they could get an entire wardrobe for pretty cheap. But Darrell? Once he was a teenager, he wanted nothing to do with that. That year he asked if he could just have his school clothes money, so I gave it to him—and he spent it all on *one* pair of special brand-new Bugle Boy jeans, which were all the rage back then.

It wasn't the choice I would have made, but he was old enough to learn how to buy clothes and learn how to budget himself, and he was so happy the day he got to wear them to school.

At home, we would say goodbye to Darrell every morning and then start our day with a walk in the park, a lesson, or one of my favorite activities: the seven-minute-story time. Teaching six kids whose ages ranged from three to eleven isn't typical for classrooms, but the method I used was to teach to the oldest in the room. That was Natalie, and whatever I taught to her, the youngest would go through all the lessons and pick up whatever they could. So, for seven-minute-story time, I would give them a writing prompt and they would have seven minutes to turn it into a story of their own making. They weren't allowed to stop writing until the seven minutes were up. The prompt might be: "It was really dark, and when I came around the corner . . . Go!" When the timer went off, they would take turns reading their stories out loud to the group. The older ones would help the younger ones, and most of our days would start with everyone laughing so hard at the crazy-funny stories they created.

At least a couple times a week we would walk to the library singing songs the whole way. All my kids were avid readers and we were always checking out a bunch of new books. At home they would have to hide books from each other because if one kid put it down, another would pick it up and start reading, and then the first kid would cry, "Who stole my book?!"

We started volunteering at the library every week too. We even did puppet shows to entertain other kids and families.

Ron had a whole garage full of tools, and we were always building and making things ourselves, so he jumped in to help build us a puppet theater. Then we all worked together to make the puppets, sew their costumes, and come up with the stories. That kept the kids involved in the community in a whole new way.

At one point we were studying outer space and their assignment was to write up a report about a particular planet to present to Ron when he got home. Sarah picked Uranus. Now, I'm a joker. But Ron is the most proper, sweet, religious kind of man you will ever meet, so when Sarah started reading: "Ur-*anus* is mostly brown. Ur-*anus* has tons of gas. Ur-*anus* . . ."

Ron turned about four shades of purple when he looked over at me as if to say, *What is happening? Did you let her do this?*

I just smiled and said, "Well, it *is* a planet."

When we studied the human body, I had each of the kids lie on the floor on a big piece of paper, and we traced their bodies. As we learned about the different organs, we drew them, and cut out and colored them and pasted them into place. We had a lot of windows in that Greenfield house, so there wasn't enough wall space to hang all those life-size body pictures up. We had to tape some of them up on the ceiling, and some of those bodies were hung above the dining room table. One night, as we were eating dinner, one of Alan's organs dropped off the ceiling and landed right onto someone's plate. "Is that liver we're having for dinner?" someone asked, and everyone broke out laughing so hard.

I tried to make everything fun, but sometimes I had to do some serious teaching about solving problems.

One of the guiding principles in our religion is that we believe families are forever. We believe we're all going to live on together, so helping each other in the family matters. It matters a lot. I told the kids over and over, "If you can't get along with the people in your living room, how are you going to get along in the world?"

Homeschooling gave me a lot of opportunities to teach that lesson over and over, like the time when two of my girls were fighting over a blanket. Both of the girls were so mad at each other because one came over and took the blanket off the other one and said it was hers. So I stepped in and said, "Girls, this is a blanket. It is just *a blanket*. I can get you another blanket, but what you have to realize is that your relationship is not worth a blanket. You have got to figure this out because nothing you do is ever going to be more important than your relationship."

When they didn't stop arguing, I said, "If you are so desperate to have this blanket, I will cut it in half. I will make each of you a blanket. I will make it as identical as I can because that relationship is important to me, and it should be important to you."

**WHEN SARAH GOT** married, somebody was passing around a book of advice, and Natalie wrote in there, "Sarah, remember it's a blanket." That made me so happy. It didn't always happen, but I tried really hard to teach my children to work together—and clearly some of it stuck!

Just being mad at each other and holding grudges was never allowed. They could have disagreements. "It is okay to disagree," I said, "but you still need to love each other in the end, because family matters more than anything else."

When we had to go places in the car sometimes, because kids are kids, somebody would start arguing. And every time I would pull over and park the car. "Mom, what are you waiting for?" someone would ask. "Well," I said, "as soon as you work this out and you're done fighting we can go. Go ahead, you can fight." Of course they would stop and tell me to keep driving, especially if we were heading to someplace fun, but if they started back up again, I'd pull right back over and park the car. I actually said, "The car won't go if you're fighting." I said it so often that some of the little ones really did believe it.

At home one time when a big fight built up between Alan and Jacob, I took a different approach. I stepped in between them and said, "All right, enough. We are going to solve this problem, and here is how: you are both going to prepare your cases and when Dad gets home, we'll have court, and he will be the judge." The other kids chose a side and then I directed them to different rooms. Their lesson that day was to literally prepare and present their case. And they had to work together to do it.

**ONE OF THE** reasons I love homeschooling is because you can change things up in the here and now, right in the moment, and adjust the lessons to whatever the children need, instead of putting them through some static expectations of learning for their assigned grade levels.

When Ron walked in the door after work, I walked right over to him and handed him my graduation robe and a wooden mallet. "You are now a judge," I said. "This is your robe and this is your mallet. Court will be in session very soon." Then I added, "And we will not be eating dinner until this case is resolved."

Ron laughed, and shook his head.

EVERY PROJECT WE DID, THE children would learn about something new, and I would learn something new about them.

That definitely held true when I taught the girls to sew.

In the 1980s, two-foot-tall muslin rabbits with pinafores were all the rage, so I decided to teach them how to make them. I figured with that one project they would learn hand sewing, machine sewing, embroidery, and everything they needed to know if they wanted to sew clothing or make projects on their own. By the time they were done, Natalie said, "Well, I'm glad I know how to do that." Sarah said, "Oh, I hope I never have to do this again in my life!" And Hillary decided to attach and reattach the head of her rabbit several times to see what he would look like with different expressions. She just loved it. She took it and ran with it, and in time I would learn that there wasn't anything that girl couldn't do, from building a brick mailbox to installing a deck to making a wedding dress.

I just loved that so much.

Another benefit of homeschooling the kids was that they had less exposure to learning bad behaviors that are a part of regular school. For example, swearing. My kids never learned to swear. They just weren't around it. But on occasion there are the unexpected influences of friends and neighbors.

One day the girls came home from a friend's house and they were all just mortified about something that had happened. "You have to tell Mom," Hillary said.

"Tell me what? What's going on?" I asked.

It was Natalie who said, "Jaime said the really bad S-word."

"The really bad S-word?" I said. "Wait a minute, *which* really bad S-word?"

"We can't say it," they said. (Good girls.)

I agreed to let them say it just this once.

"Shut up!" Sarah said, and then she covered her mouth with her hands.

"Jaime said 'shut up' at her house," Natalie explained.

I could barely hold back my laughter.

Then I had to explain it to them: "That's a bad word that we do not allow in *our* family, because we feel it shows disrespect toward others, and in our home we believe that nothing is more important than your relationships. But sometimes in other families they have a different set of rules."

All "swearing" exposure aside, I loved having the kids' friends over to our house, and there were so many kids in our area who had two parents working full-time that we ended up with a full house almost every day after school. I didn't mind; the more the merrier. We'd serve them fruit punch and homemade cookies that the kids baked themselves. I pretty much became known as the Kool-Aid mom (even though we couldn't afford real Kool-Aid and used some generic "mix-aid" instead).

With all those mouths to feed, my seven kids and at least seven friends over on many days, we needed really big batches of inexpensive snacks. So I invented a recipe called Doans' Big Batch Cookies. The dough is made in a really big bowl, sometimes with up to a dozen eggs and six cups of oats and eight cups flour. It's a really huge recipe that is quite adaptable. (I've included it at the end of the book!) And we made a lot of bread at home, too, but about every six weeks, my hand mixer would break, and we had to go out and buy a new mixer. So I decided that we needed a big mixer. We needed a restaurant-size mixer. And the one I wanted? A KitchenAid. Well, I found out that they cost over $200, and my first thought was, *There's no way we're getting a restaurant-size mixer.*

But it didn't take long before I got into the mindset that we could figure it out.

We were in the car when I noticed there was a whole lot of building going on right around our town. I turned off the road and drove down to one of those construction sites and I offered to do some work for them—to clean up the houses once they were done building them.

They said "yes."

Whenever a construction crew was finished, they would give me a call, and I would gather up all the children and we would go down to clean that house as a family. With all those hands working together, it didn't take us very long. We got about twenty dollars a house, and we saved that twenty dollars and then waited for the next one. By the end of the summer, we had made enough to buy that KitchenAid.

On the day we brought it home, we all celebrated with a special Doans' Big Batch, and from then on, every time we needed to mix things, we could turn on the mixer and it would work. Every time. I just loved that.

**THEY MIGHT NOT** have realized it at the time, but I think the kids learned something special about working together on those cleaning jobs: many hands make light work. And after we bought that mixer, which made our Doans' Big Batch recipes so much easier to make, they also learned a lesson about having the right tools for the job.

I have to say, that mixer was a good investment, because Josh still has the KitchenAid—and, as of 2021, it's still running!

I didn't take work outside the home often, but when I did, I tried to include my children. I knew they needed to learn to work hard, to work together, to appreciate things, and to take good care of things. Most importantly, what I wanted to show them is that if they really wanted something, if they set their minds on it and worked hard, they could get it. Whatever it was, they could do it. And I encouraged them to come up with their own ideas, and to try.

9

# Not in the
# Mother's Handbook

Every spring, we held the Doansbury Family Bake-Off. (*Doans*bury, like Pillsbury.)

It started off as just a family thing, where everyone would bake a secret recipe, and we'd place all the treats on the table, and then we'd judge whose cookies, or cupcakes, or other dessert was the best. The kids were all so creative. And each piece was numbered, so nobody knew whose was whose or who made what, and it turned into a big important title for whoever won. Everyone had to plan ahead of time and submit a list of ingredients. Then we had to schedule time in the kitchen so no one would peek in and see.

This tradition started before we moved to Greenfield, and it was such a hit that the second time we did it, we invited my parents, my grandmother, and my sister and brother to be the judges. The kids made special judge badges for them to wear, and every year the competition got a little bit more intense. My mother had an old mimeograph machine (if you don't know, that's like an olden-day hand-cranked copy machine), and we made flyers, and judging sheets, and the kids came up with all sorts of different categories: best flavor, best color, best appearance, most refreshing. So everybody would win at least one category. But Best Overall Dessert won the grand prize, and the kids went crazy for it. They wanted that little plastic trophy or whatever prize we came up with so much. I think Alan won the first year, and my Frosty Strawberry Bars won another year. (I've included this recipe at the end of the book too!)

NOT LONG AFTER WE MOVED to Greenfield, my parents moved to Oregon, up near where my younger sister had moved. Sadly that meant they couldn't be our judges anymore. So we invited a couple of church families to come out and judge the bake-off. That upped everyone's game, because now it wasn't just family. This was a *real* competition.

Oh, it was fun. Simple, good, tasty fun.

Our Christmases were so much fun too. As you can imagine, they didn't involve a lot of store-bought gifts. At one point, to save money, we told the children that we were no longer buying Christmas presents at all, but everybody had to make their own presents to exchange. We truly stuck to it, and it became like the bake-off. They would talk about their ideas, get their supplies, hide their materials so no one would see, and they would work, and they would paint, and they would ask for alone time in the garage. Josh was maybe three or four the very first year, and he didn't know what to do. So I said, "Let's make cookies and you can wrap them up, and everybody can have a cookie." And he made gingerbread cookies, and everybody loved that.

Jake could build anything, and one year he came up with an original idea for a manual gumball machine, built out of a base of wood with a piece that slid in and out to release the gumballs from an upside-down quart jar. It was so cool, we probably could have built lots of them and sold them. One year Alan made a miniature basketball-hoop game with a little catapult, and you'd put a little bead in and it would shoot over into the net. Natalie carved Dala horses for everybody and painted them. They're Swedish horse figures, and they say you're not a good Swede unless you have a herd. I've got a pretty good-size herd now.

All the kids just put in so much effort and we had so much fun with it. I don't think they missed having store-bought Christmas presents at all.

Occasionally, Santa would gift them with some big surprise, like new bikes—meaning old cast-off bikes that Ron fixed up and painted. And one year Ron and I did get them a Nintendo. The kids went absolutely wild. I think it was ten times as special for them because they weren't expecting it. We kept it in the room near the garage, hooked up to our old thirteen-inch TV, so it wouldn't take over our lives. They enjoyed it when we let them play it, but they seemed happy to go back to reading and making things for themselves when we didn't.

Christmas Eve is the bigger holiday in the Swedish tradition, and we always held a Smorgasbord no matter what kind of a year we were having. We just adjusted the feast to our budget, and to our tastes.

My parents raised us with strict rules about what had to be in the Smorgasbord. There had to be seven types of cookies, which was easy, and three different kinds of fish, even though I'm not a fish lover. My whole life they would serve lutefisk or some other seafood dishes I didn't like. So, at my house, I used Swedish Fish—you know, the chewy red candy—and a bowl full of Goldfish crackers, and bowl full of pretzel Goldfish. I used a can of tuna one year to show that my three types of "fish" were covered.

My mother laughed and said, "Jenny, you are *terrible!*"

We'd have rice pudding, and pork, and *dopp i gryta* (dip-in-the-pot)—a traditional dish that's like a sausage broth that you dip rye bread into. It's delicious, and one of Ron's favorites. But it's meant to represent the "lean times," when families only had bread and broth to eat. And we weren't far from it!

There were Swedish meatballs, of course, and lots of cheeses. And Christmas slush, one of my mother's favorites, which was frozen pineapple, bananas, and orange juice mixed with soda, served in this big copper punch bowl.

We made all kinds of desserts out of whatever we had in the cupboard, and we were basically baking for a week. So many of the ingredients were inexpensive—rice, potatoes, flour—and we made the most of whatever we had. So it wasn't spendy, but it always, *always* felt special.

Some years we went out Christmas caroling, and after that, everyone would get to open one gift. It was pajamas. Always pajamas. They expected it. I made everyone matching pajamas to wear to bed and to wear on Christmas morning.

And then we read *The Night Before Christmas* to the kids before they went to bed.

Life at the Doan family home was *good*. Ron and I made sure of it.

BY THE MID-1990S, LIFE OUTSIDE of our four walls was changing. And that seemed to be out of our hands.

One day I happened to see a drug exchange go down behind the bush in our front yard. I called the police. I'm not a coward.

But then, not long after that, some guys came in and robbed us, and took our Nintendo. The kids didn't believe it at first. I'd disconnected it from the TV so many times, they thought I'd just hidden it from them!

Thankfully, the police caught the perpetrators. They had broken in and stolen from nearly every home on our street. The police even recovered some of the stolen goods. One day a police officer called me and said, "We need you to come down and identify this Nintendo." And I said, "How am I going to know it's mine? It looks like everybody else's Nintendo."

"We need you to identify this as yours so that we can charge the culprit," they said, implying that I should identify it as mine even if I wasn't sure. But I couldn't do that. I could never tell a lie like that. I said, "Well, I'll come look at it, but I'm not gonna identify it as mine unless I *know* that it's mine." So I went down to the station and looked at it and thought, *Well, it* looks *like our Nintendo. It's kind of gray and black. But who knows?* Then I pushed a button and the lid came up, and there was a game disc in there that said "Doan" right across it, in permanent marker.

"Yes, this is mine," I said.

"How do you know?"

"Look right there," I said. "There is your evidence. I can safely say that this is my Nintendo."

I was thankful we got the kids' Nintendo back, once they were done using it as evidence. It was mostly a good community with *many* good kids. But witnessing a drug deal and getting robbed was unnerving.

Our frayed nerves weren't helped by the fact that when it came to money, we were drowning.

Owning a home and having a mortgage wasn't everything we thought it would be. Interest rates skyrocketed and our monthly payments grew much higher than we ever expected.

With Ron spending more money than ever on gas for his long commute, and seven growing kids in the house eating food faster than we could prepare it, our budgets were stretched about as thin as could be. It's not like I could just go out and get a job to fix this. There is no way to pay for daycare for seven children and make a wage that's worthwhile. Especially doing a job that I was qualified to do, which would have been a shop clerk or a teacher's aide. It's not like I was gonna get a job as a rocket scientist. Plus, I was homeschooling the kids—and the kids needed me.

Our youngest, Josh, was barely five years old that summer. I was helping him put his shirt on, and as he held his tiny arms up over his head, my thumb ran into a lump on his arm. I stopped and looked at it, and touched it again, and it felt like a golf ball in his upper arm.

It's hard to describe the fear that shot through me. Most of my children had never been to a doctor in all of their lives. For one, we couldn't afford it, but they also were really healthy kids. And when they weren't, for the most part I could fix 'em or mend 'em myself pretty well. But this? Josh needed a doctor. We took him to the hospital, and they determined it was a tumor in his lymph gland. It needed to come out. He needed surgery, and they wanted to operate right away.

Life gets really muddled when your kid gets sick.

That night, I thought I would die in my sleep of a broken heart. But the next morning I got up, I took care of the kids, I did the dishes. And the next morning, we took Josh into the hospital for surgery. They dressed him in a hospital-issued gown, and he was so excited when he saw that it was covered in Mickey Mouse designs. Here my heart was breaking, because we didn't know what they were going to find once they wheeled him into surgery, and he was laughing and joyful.

Ron and I tried not ever to scare him or make him feel like he needed to worry. It was just, "Well, we'd better go to the doctor and check this out." And he was still smiling when they wheeled him in. But Ron and I went out to the car and just cried in each other's arms while we waited. I didn't know what we were going to do if this didn't go the way we hoped it would go. We just prayed that our littlest boy would be okay.

The doctors removed the tumor, and Josh came through fine, but they never determined whether that tumor was cancerous or not. They said it could have been brought on by something as simple as a cat scratch, but we didn't own a cat. They said we should "watch him." And we did. And thankfully, whatever it was, it never came back.

But Josh's triple-bad summer was just beginning. A couple of weeks later, he tried to climb the fence in the backyard, and he fell. There was a nail sticking out and it ripped through the palm of his hand. That led to another trip to the doctor, and stitches.

A week or so after that, Josh wanted to get out of the house, so I let him go in the backyard again. "No climbing fences!" I said, and he agreed. When I checked on him, he was sitting quietly in the grass, petting the dog.

Alan was mowing the front yard at the time.

That's when I heard the kind of blood-curdling scream a mother never wants to hear.

It came from the backyard. Seconds later, Josh came running into the house crying, "Owww. Owwww!"

"What happened?!" I asked. That's when I saw the blood— and the screwdriver in his hand.

Alan came running in and saw his brother, and quickly realized what had happened. He had found one of Ron's big screwdrivers on the ground, he said, and didn't want to run it over with the mower. So without really thinking about it, he picked it up and launched it over the house and into the backyard.

It landed, pointy side down, on Josh's head.

I thought, *This is not in the mother's handbook.*

The screwdriver didn't break his skull, thank goodness. It only split the skin, but it was still very scary.

Up until this point, Ron and I had been able to manage our money. We didn't have money to save, and we didn't have much money to spend, but through the grace of God we kept going. We were able to live, you know? But now we had a whole lot of unexpected medical bills.

I tried to figure it out. I wrote letters to everybody explaining our situation, with seven kids and the back-to-back accidents, asking, "Please forgive this debt." And some did, but not everybody did, and it was a *huge* amount of debt.

Trying to pay debt over here meant going into more debt over there. We were robbing Peter to pay Paul, and it wasn't working.

This was before Dave Ramsey was on the radio. But somehow we heard about debt counseling. The idea of it was you could go in and talk to an attorney, and he would evaluate your finances. He was supposed to say something like, "All right, I think this is the best thing for you. You can do this and you can do that to eliminate this debt over time," and you would pay a fee for him to do that. So we tried that. And the guy we went to took one look at our finances and said, "I don't even know how you're living. I don't know how you make it day-to-day. How are you feeding your family? You don't have a food budget on here."

I told him, "Well, I can everything. All kinds of things. Last week we were following a broccoli truck and a case of broccoli fell off. I stopped and picked up that case when they just drove on. They didn't know it fell, so I picked it up and took it home.

And I made broccoli soup, broccoli bread, broccoli casserole. I ground it up. I put it in everything. Everything I could think to do with that, I did. After the third day the kids were like, 'We cannot eat any more broccoli.' So I said to my children, and this is a quote, 'You go to your room and you pray to love broccoli and don't come out till you do, because it's all we have.' And, obviously, we didn't starve to death, you know?"

The debt counselor said he saw no choice but for us to declare bankruptcy.

That summer, there were times when as a family we would kneel down and we would pray: "We've done everything we know how to do, and we need help." And every time, within a couple of days, somebody would tape a hundred-dollar bill to our front door, and we'd go to the store and buy groceries; or I'd get a phone call from a friend saying, "My apple tree is going nuts. Do you want some?" And we'd make apple pie filling and applesauce to our heart's delight.

I never stopped believing that we would be okay.

We were always helping others, so other people would always help us.

My mother used to say, "When you cast your bread upon the water, it comes back buttered. There's enough for everybody." It means that because you've given something away, now you're going to get more, and I believe this with all my heart. It's how we made it this far as a family, and it's ultimately how we would grow our business many years in the future.

But financially speaking, at that point, we were so far behind. Literally, we had nothing. We thought we had no choice but to declare bankruptcy, and we were trying to sort through how to do that just as Ron turned forty. Forty was a big deal for him. He started to wonder, *What am I doing?* All of a sudden he was saying things like, "We don't have to live here."

"What do you mean we don't have to live here?" I asked. "In Greenfield?"

"Yeah," he said.

"Where would we go?"

Praying had always been a part of our marriage, so together and separately, we both started praying about it. And we started to get some answers.

At first I thought maybe we could move to Sacramento, to where my older sister lived. I'd get to be closer to her, and it was a much a bigger community with more opportunities.

We knew a guy from our church who was the head of hiring for the Quaker Oats people. They had a factory up there. And Ron being a machinist, he could get a job anywhere. One of his missionary friends had a construction company up there, too, so we thought they might be able to build us a house to suit our family. The more we talked about it, the more we kept trying to piece it all together.

I finally took a drive up to Sacramento just to see the place and to work on some of the details, but hardly any of the things we hoped would happen were working out in real life. Our house wasn't selling. Our connections weren't coming together. And I found myself driving along in prayer.

Car prayers are a thing with me. When I'm in the car alone, that's when I talk to God. About everything.

"I just don't know what it is we're supposed to do," I said, "and I don't know why everything's not falling into place. We know the perfect people. We can have a house built. Why isn't our house selling? Our house should sell so we can do this, and the kids can do this, and there's a college right there so Darrell won't have to move far away for college." I asked God, "Why aren't things falling into place?"

And into my mind, as if someone spoke to me, I heard the words, *Because I want you to go to Missouri.*

It was so strange! I had never had that kind of experience before. I said right out loud, "Who said anything about going to Missouri? I am going to Sacramento!"

And I had the feeling again: *I would really like you to move your family to Missouri.*

I was stunned. I thought, *What the heck? Missouri?* We didn't know anybody there. *Nobody.* We had never been there, and didn't know a thing about it.

When I came home from my weekend trip where nothing was working out, I walked in and called out, "Ron, I'm home."

"Hey, how are you doing?" he shouted back. Ron was out in the garage in his workshop. So I came around the corner and said to him, "Ron, I think we're supposed to move to Missouri."

He was busy working on something at his workbench, but he whirled around and looked me in the face and said, "I know."

"You *know?*" I said. "How do you know?"

"I've had that feeling the whole time you've been gone, that we're supposed to take our family and move to Missouri."

"Where would we go?" I asked, and Ron pulled out an old map, opened it up, and randomly put his finger on it.

"We will go right here," he said.

"What is *there?*" I asked.

He moved his finger and we saw that he'd landed in what looked like the middle of nowhere, near a little town called Hamilton.

10

# We're Not in California Anymore

When you come to a prayerful decision, it doesn't always remove all the doubt from your mind. So you have to do the bottom line.

Ask yourself: *What's the worst that could happen?*

When it came to making a move to Missouri, I figured the bottom line was this: we would go there, we might hate it, we would come back. I mean, that's about it.

"So if we get there and it's a terrible idea, we won't have to stay," I said.

"Sure," Ron replied.

At this point we weren't going anywhere, because our house hadn't sold yet. At the time, my parents were living in Oregon. So I said to Ron, "My parents are thinking about going on a mission, so maybe we could go and live in their house for a couple of years, save up some money, get ahead, and see how it goes.

We could see if we do okay with a big move, you know? We're homeschooling our children, so that won't matter, and they love it at my parents' house."

He agreed, as he has with just about every idea I've ever offered. That was Ron. So we packed up the kids and some of our most precious possessions, put everything else we owned into storage, and drove up to my parents' house in Oregon. But by the time we got there, they had decided not to go on the mission.

I think they thought we had lost our minds.

So, in 1994, Ron and I and six of our kids (Darrell had already moved out and gone to college by then) moved ourselves and our most precious possessions to Oregon—into my youngest sister's basement in Salem.

By "most precious possessions," I mean things like Alan's baseball card collection, which he had been collecting all his life. I don't know if it was worth anything, but it was the most precious thing to him. I had my guitars. I had my plants. (I always had a green thumb.) I kept a couple of pieces of furniture that were really, really important to me as well, and each of our children kept what they thought was most important to them. We kept those things with us instead of putting them in storage, specifically so they would be safe—but over the next six months, my sister's basement flooded. Five times.

We'd wake up in the middle of the night and find ourselves ankle-deep in water, thinking, *What is going on here?*

My sister couldn't understand it. They'd lived in that house for years without a problem. "We've never had a basement flood!" she said.

Ron was gone a lot, working hard so we could save, so a lot of that time it was just me and the kids in that basement. After the first flood or two, I painted a whole big wall down there. I wrote on the top, "I'm thankful for . . ." and I hung a pen and I said,

"We can't let this negativity get to us, so everybody write on this wall the things that we have to be thankful for."

We did the best we could.

"I'm thankful for the sunshine." "I'm thankful for my brother." "I'm thankful for the house, because at least we have a roof over our head!" "I'm thankful for our family."

We tried to be thankful for whatever it was we had left.

I've always been a big proponent of gratitude. No matter how rough your situation is, there's somebody that has it worse. And no matter how bad it is, we can't live in that sorry place, feeling sorry for ourselves all the time.

Writing on that thankful wall helped. It really did.

Then, one Sunday, we were standing in water, again, when somebody came in wearing church clothes and water boots and put a sump pump in for us. But it wasn't enough. It still flooded.

I finally said to Ron, "All right. This is like Jonah in the whale. We're being swallowed alive down here! We better go to Missouri."

It was time to take the leap of faith that God had asked us to take.

———

As we gathered up what little we had left, we talked to the kids about Missouri. Most of the things they knew they had learned from our homeschool lessons, or things they read in certain history novels. Because of that, they thought our move would be a big adventure, like we were going back in time to the days of Daniel Boone and Davy Crockett, and maybe even the Wild West. They assumed we'd have to learn to hunt and fish, because that's how people got food in those days. We had never done anything like that. As far as our kids were concerned, fish came from the supermarket, not from a body of water. They were scared, but mostly they were excited.

On February 23, 1995, I wrote in my journal:

*Tomorrow we are moving to Missouri. The truck will come, and we will drive away. I can hardly believe that we have been living in this basement for six months. I am sad and happy to leave but most of all scared, but I am not taking counsel from my fears. I am trying to do what the heavenly Father wants me to do. I'm trying to do the Lord's will. The bishop said, "When the Lord gets us where he wants us, he will prosper us." I hope Missouri is the place. We have given up so much, yet here we are. We're still willing to give up for whatever the Lord requires of us. We love the Lord.*

*The children are anxious, scared, willing, and worried. Everything we own fits in a little truck. We are going to Missouri. Wow. So many people have been so kind to me and helped us. The women all signed a pillow for me, and Jeanette Elliot gave me a little sculpture she made.*

*Tammy Parent made me a quilt. She saw in a dream that I needed comfort, and in the dream I was wrapped in this quilt surrounded by music. So she began to make a quilt for me and wrote the words to hymns in squares all over the quilt.*

*Brother Randolph wrote us a letter. Sister Carlisle wrote us a letter, sent thank-yous, muffins, blueberries, and we gave them our rabbit and our love.*

*Sister Celia Slack has been teaching us how to crochet. She gave us an afghan. She gave Sarah a little gold footprint necklace, Hillary a gold chain, Natalie a Christmas pendant necklace, and she gave us her love and a wonderful skill. Brother Goumand helped fix my dresser. Susie Pederson gave me crochet instructions. Things are almost ready for moving. I have to get a bumper for my van. Ron won a $25 gift certificate two weeks in a row at work.*

Natalie had just gotten her license, so we made the trip in two cars and a U-Haul that was towing a third car. We didn't know anything about snow when we put her in one of those cars to drive across the middle of the United States in late February. We just thought, *Are you gonna be a little cold?* Not, *Are you going to die?*

Along the way, the snow in the headlights was coming at us so hard and fast, it looked like a scene from *Star Wars*, like we were making the jump to lightspeed. We couldn't see a thing! We had to pull off to the side because our big giant van was sliding off the road. But then on the side of the road we were scared that another car or big truck would come barreling down the road and slide right into *us*. All night I worried, "Are we gonna die?"

Looking back on it now, I think, *Holy smoke, I can't believe we did that.*

But the snow stopped, and we finally made it to the outskirts of Hamilton on March 2, 1995. All we saw were farms and fields. There was nothing there! I put on a really good face, but I kept thinking, *Oh my gosh. What have we done?*

In the morning, I went over to the U-Haul to check on my plants. I'd kept beautiful plants ever since Ron and I were married, and thankfully I'd kept them upstairs at my sister's house, so they had survived the floods. But I opened the back of the U-Haul and they were all melted.

When potted plants freeze, they turn to sludge. I didn't know that. All my plants were dead, and I cried again: "God, this is not what I planned." But the kids didn't know. They were still on their big adventure, and I didn't want to ruin it for them. So I hid my tears and tried to trust that somehow we were still doing the right thing.

We decided to drive a little farther, and soon we discovered the center of town, with an old-fashioned-looking main street full of storefronts. There was a bank, and a church, and a little grocery store. I had called ahead and spoken to a realtor in town, but I didn't see a real estate office anywhere. I asked around and someone told us, "Oh, that's over on McGaughy." So we went over to McGaughy Street, and it wasn't an office. It was the man's house. So I knocked on his door, and I said to the man who answered, "Are you a realtor?"

"Well, from time to time I do some real estate deals," he said.

"Okay! I'm Jenny Doan. I called you earlier, about moving from California. We need a rental."

"That would take me about a week."

A *week*?

"Well, can you point me to a hotel?" I asked.

"Oh my," he said. "There are no hotels here."

My mind started churning over what we were going to do to fix this.

But then, the man said, "Don't worry. You can just stay with us."

Now, if this had happened in California I never would have considered it. But somehow, I was desperate enough and tired enough, and he seemed friendly enough, that this sounded like a really good idea to me. This man had a three-bedroom home, and I think he and his wife had nine children. We walked in with our six kids and I said to them, "Be friends."

That family was sleeping two to a bed already, and at first the kids were like, "We cannot stay here." But as soon as those kids started talking to each other, I swear they became instant friends. It was Hillary's birthday that day, and as soon as they found out, those kids invited a whole bunch of their friends over just to celebrate. They sang "Happy Birthday" to her.

I looked at Ron as they all ran and played together, and I said, "Ron. We're not in California anymore."

———

We stayed with that family for nearly a week. They fed us. They pulled mattresses out from under beds for us. They took care of us and asked nothing in return.

It was snowing when they showed us a little blue house up the street that we could rent for next to nothing. It was rough. It had plywood floors. No appliances. The plaster walls were cracked, with big holes in them. It literally had a sapling growing through the shower in the bathroom, and the entire place was full of trash.

My kids looked at that broken-down house and said, "All right, Mom, we've done some crazy things, but this? We can't do this."

"Sure, we can," I said. "We can do this. And it'll be fun!"

We took bags and bags of trash out and started to clean the house all up.

We didn't have electricity or a fridge in the first week, so we kept a cooler outside for our milk and cold food. There was one bedroom downstairs, where Ron and I slept, and we thought we would put the children upstairs in the big attic area. But someone had blown insulation into it, so in order to make a place for our kids to sleep, we had to take all of that insulation out of the house in garbage bags too. I'll admit it was horrible, but it was only for a short time while we looked for another place to live.

For the kids, it really was like living in the Wild West. They were fascinated when I bought milk from a farmer and we had to scrape the cream off the top. We had never done that before. The boys learned new skills from Ron as he repaired the windows and fixed the roof, and then they built their very own tree house in a big old tree in the yard.

Since spring was on the way, pretty soon I was able to hang our clothes outside on a clothesline. I loved that. Then we had someone come by and plow a spot in the yard so we could make a little garden, and we started to look at seed catalogues, imagining all the good things we could grow if we ended up staying in that house longer than we planned.

Before long, we put floors in the whole place, including the top floor. And when Hillary knocked over a gallon of paint on the new dining room floor, we didn't get upset. We just painted the whole floor to match.

I don't think many renters put so much effort into fixing up their rental homes, but Ron always said, "It doesn't matter where we live, we're going to leave it better than when we came."

Ron started looking for work in Kansas City because the pay there was much higher, which meant we'd be able to save a lot faster for a bigger place.

He got connected to a man at our church who ran a machinist department, so I called him up and asked, "Where would you like me to send a hard copy of my husband's resume?" He responded, "Any man that would let his wife do his job hunting for him isn't worth hiring. You can tell him to forget it."

I was shocked. It was a wake-up call for what we were coming into out here. It felt like we had stepped back in time.

Ron found work pretty fast at a factory in Chillicothe, though, without the higher pay or a long commute. And we started going to church on Sundays, where the kids made even more instant friends. Everyone was so welcoming.

Right away, a man at church came up to me and said, "I got a bunch of hogs at an auction. I wanted to know if you wanted one."

I said, "Awesome. Well, how much is it?"

"Well, the hogs are five dollars, but you gotta pay for the processing."

"That's okay," I said.

I didn't have any idea what "the processing" was or what it would cost, but I figured we could figure that out.

Then I told Ron, "That guy over there, he got us a hog in an auction."

And Ron got very excited.

"He got us a *motorcycle?*" he said.

"No, no, not a motorcycle. It's a pig-hog. And it's only five dollars, but we have to pay for the processing, or do it ourselves."

"Oh well, that's great," he said. "Five dollars for a whole hog?"

We were all excited to get a selection of bacon, and roast, and pork loin . . . and then we got a call from the man who sold it to us, and he said, "Well, I got some bad news for you. Your hog fell off the truck. And he broke his leg."

"Hmm," I said. "First of all, how do you know it was *my* hog?"

He didn't answer that question.

He said, "Now, when that happens, the adrenaline rushes and it makes the meat really tough. So, basically, the only thing you can get out of this hog is sausage."

We ended up with three hundred pounds of pork sausage.

It turns out pork sausage goes really well with biscuits and gravy, and I'd never eaten biscuits and gravy before, but I quickly became a master biscuit maker and a gravy connoisseur.

Everything like that was so bizarrely funny to us.

ONE NIGHT, BEFORE THE WORK on the house was finished, we had about ten kids over to visit. They wanted to watch movies, but our living room was too small and still full of boxes. So we put our old thirteen-inch TV outside, put blankets on the lawn, and did an outdoor movie theater. The kids all loved it—our kids and their new friends too.

Time felt like it slowed down in Missouri. And because of that, everything we did felt more important. I'm not sure why it felt that way, but it did.

In California, if you saw someone in a grocery store, the chance of seeing them again in your life was pretty rare. Here, we ran into the same people all the time. Everybody knew everybody. They really were your neighbors.

When I came out of the grocery store in Hamilton one day, before I knew everybody myself, I unlocked my car and the boy carrying my groceries said, "You must not be from here."

"How can you tell?" I asked.

"No one locks their doors here," he said.

I stopped locking my car at the grocery store after that.

Not long after, I noticed there was a community theater in town, so I stopped by to volunteer. "I have a theater background," I told the folks inside. "I can sing, and I sew. I could be your costumer."

An older woman looked at me and said, "We only do one show a year. We don't need a costumer."

"But I love to sew. So if you need any help—"

"Well, if you love to sew, you could take a quilting class," she said.

I thought to myself, *I'm pretty sure that old people do that. I don't want to do that. But thanks anyway.* I wished them well, and I went home.

AFTER A FEW MONTHS OF searching for a bigger place to live, I still hadn't found anything much bigger in downtown Hamilton, so I went out driving the country roads on the outskirts, looking for someplace that might not be listed. Eventually I came across an old farmhouse in the middle of nowhere. The land around it was beautiful, but the house looked like it had been abandoned for a long time. The grass was right up to the windows. The porch was sinking. Some windows were broken. The paint was more chipped than it was white.

*Perfect!* I thought.

I went to the county courthouse and got a plot map so I could see who owned that property, and I found out it was owned by a man named Courtney Diddle. So I gave him a call.

"You have a house that's sitting empty," I said, "and I'd like to know if you'd be willing to rent that house."

"No," he said. "My dad died there. We're just gonna let it fall down."

"Please don't let it fall down," I said. "It's beautiful!"

"Well, what do you bring to the table if I let you rent this?" he asked.

And I don't know where these words came from, but I said to him, "I'll tell you what. I'll give you everything I've got. I'll fill that house with a family."

He fell silent.

After a long pause, he said, "Maybe I should come meet you."

# Farm Friends & Fishing Poles

I t turned out Mr. Diddle was a very religious man. He wanted to pray with us. So we stood in a circle, held hands, and prayed. Then he said, "You know what? I feel like you're supposed to be in that house."

So we made a deal. We would work for our rent. We would fix up the house for him instead of paying him cash. We had to show him, receipt-wise, enough investment in paint and materials to total what the rent might've been every month. And Mr. Diddle went from wishing his empty old house would just fall down to being super excited about what was happening to it. He even came down and helped us put a fence around the house the first weekend we moved in, so the cows in the area wouldn't come walking right up to our windows.

The farmhouse, which was built in the 1800s, was surrounded by over two hundred acres of land. While it wasn't the prettiest house ever on the inside, the way it functioned on the outside was genius. They had a windmill that drove water up a hill, where it filled a big concrete, rock-lined reservoir up on the rise, kind of like a big swimming pool. Gravity would feed it down to the house, which meant we had the best water pressure ever.

Some of the water was collected off a spring, but the house was also crisscrossed with gutters, and all those gutters ran into two cisterns. I looked into it all and said to the kids, "They didn't even bring electricity to the house until 1967, but they had this advanced system of water moving and collection. Isn't that interesting?"

I suppose some kids might have rolled their eyes. But not mine. They were genuinely excited about our new adventure. "This house is over a hundred years old," I told them. "Somebody has lived in here, and lived on this land, and survived here, for more than a *hundred years*! And now we get to learn how they did it."

Fall was coming on fast. Seasons were new to us, and the nights were already getting cold, so we bought a little woodstove at a garage sale, which they called *tag sales* here. Ron hooked it up, and then the boys went out looking for wood. When they couldn't find much around the house, Alan got out the only portable power-saw we owned, a Skil saw, and put a long extension cord on it. Then he climbed up in the trees in the yard and started cutting down limbs to use for firewood. We're lucky he didn't cut off one of his *own* limbs.

Just before the sun went down, we lit a fire in that woodstove—and the whole house filled up with smoke. So we opened up the windows and doors and sat outside on the porch, freezing to death until the smoke cleared. Then we went back in and tried to relight the fire, and it happened again. Happened the next day, and the next too. We thought there must be something wrong with that darn stove. We tried everything we could think of and we could not figure out what we were doing wrong.

That's when a thin older man with a little gray beard showed up at our door.

"All right. We've had our fun," he said. "We've been laughing at you for two weeks. We'll help you now."

He had brought us a wagon-full of wood on the back of his tractor.

I didn't know anything about wood, so I said, "Well, I don't know if this wood is any different than our wood."

And he said, "You have to let it *dry*."

We had no idea that green wood smoked. We had no idea that wood had to dry for a whole season, sometimes longer, before it was ready to burn.

This man's trailer was full of properly dried wood.

And that was how we met our neighbor Ralph who would soon become one of our dearest friends. He lived in the farmhouse just across the gravel road, and by the end of our first conversation, I was pretty sure I could learn everything I would ever need to know about farm living from Ralph.

I definitely had a lot to learn.

———

On the country roads in the Midwest, I observed that there were usually two houses across the street from each other, and then another couple of miles of wide open farmland before there were another two houses. I'm pretty sure they built them that way so the farmers could look out for each other, because in the olden days it was a long journey on horseback to get to a town.

In some ways, it was still a long journey by car.

Most of the roads out there are gravel over dirt. When it rains, they tend to fill up with water and basically turn to mud. So there are big tractors that come out and spread more gravel whenever it rains, because otherwise everyone would be driving in mud, and that's bad—as we found out firsthand not long after we moved in.

As we came across the bridge over Shoal Creek, the van got caught in the mud and slid down the gravel, rolled upside down, and landed on its roof at the bottom of the embankment. The back door fell open, so I was able to get all the children out by crawling out the back window, and nobody got hurt, but we were all kind of crying because we were so scared.

The farmhouse was only about half a mile away, so I decided we would go get Ron to help us. He was working nights then, so I knew he was home sleeping.

We started walking along the side of the road and these three men in a pickup truck pulled up beside us. They all had to be in their sixties or seventies, which seemed really old to me then (I was just thirty-seven), and they had long gray beards and hair that came past their shoulders. Their shirts were unbuttoned down to their navels, so they were bare-chested, and each one of them was holding a rifle. For a moment I thought, *Oh my gosh, I'm walking into a scene from* Deliverance.

One of them spoke out to me from the window. He said, "Ma'am, we saw your car over there. Can we help you?"

I shook my head and said, "No. No, we're fine, thank you. We're fine."

But they didn't leave. That pickup truck followed us all the way to our farmhouse and then turned right into our driveway.

*Oh my gosh, we are going to wind up on the six o'clock news,* I thought. *They're going to shoot us.*

I ran in and told Ron what happened: "We rolled the car, and these *guys* are following us."

"Is everyone okay?" Ron asked.

"Yes. For now," I said, motioning toward the men who were now getting out of their truck.

Ron picked up the phone and called the sheriff. He told him that we had an accident. He said, "Everyone's okay, but do we need to report this?"

In California you always reported when you had an accident, even if you were the only car involved. Ron didn't know if a rollover in these parts was just the sort of thing that called for a tractor and a tow rope, you know?

Ron didn't seem to understand what I was saying, though, because he didn't say anything about those men! I looked again, and these guys were now right up on our porch, and I'm think-ing, *This is it.*

"Is that the sheriff on the phone?" one of the guys said.

I noticed he only had one arm.

"Let me talk to him," he said.

Ron cautiously stretched out his arm and handed the phone to the one-armed man, and the guy said, "Hey, Sheriff, it's Lefty. These are real good people out here. They flipped their van on the embankment and they're gonna need your help."

It turned out Lefty had gone to school with the sheriff, and they were the nicest guys. Everybody truly knew *everybody* here.

―――――

L ike most of the farmers in the area, Ralph was a dairyman whose family had owned his property since it was ownable. But years before we moved there, all the big companies who used to collect milk from the small family farms decided that they weren't worth the trouble, so they stopped sending trucks out to this part of Missouri. For most of the farmers, their whole livelihood was gone.

Ralph didn't know how to be anything other than a dairy farmer, he said, so he stayed on the family farm and did the best he could. He now raised cattle to sell and kept one dairy cow for himself.

Ralph dressed the way you might expect a dairy farmer to dress, right down to his Wellies, the tall rubber boots that farmers wear. He had a car he bought in the 1950s that only had 11,000 miles on it, because he and his wife rarely went anywhere. It was a whole different mindset. And he might not have had much, but he had the most precious gift in the world: time.

On sunny days I'd say, "Let's have a picnic today, Ralph. Do you have time?"

"Oh yeah," he'd say. "We've got time. We can milk in the morning, milk in the night."

He had a flatbed wagon he hooked on the tractor. We'd put all of our picnic foods on there, then get on the wagon, and he'd drive us down through the field, through two creeks and behind a grove of trees, where it felt like we were in another world. We couldn't see any roads from that spot. We were in the middle of the wilderness. We'd have the picnic on the edge of a creek and look out over the land, and it was like living in a piece of heaven.

Ralph loved our big family. He enjoyed seeing all these kids running around. I think it brought some new fun to his life. And the kids, especially Josh, loved to work with Ralph on his farm.

One day, the kids came running up to me and said, "We're gonna go fishing!"

"Fishing? You're gonna go fishing?" I said.

And with all the confidence in the world they said, "Yeah, we're gonna go fishin'!" So I stood there with Ron, on the gravel road in front of the farmhouse, and watched our kids walk away with some of their new friends. A bunch of them had fishing poles up on their shoulders. And I looked over at Ron and I said, "Look where we live."

Ron looked at me, and I started whistling the theme to the old Andy Griffith show, and we laughed.

In California, I was such an oddball. I had this big family. I canned. I sewed. I had a garden at home. I was just an *oddball*. Then we came to Missouri and I saw how these other families lived, and I said to my husband, "Honey, I think I'm a slacker. Almost everybody has more children than we do!"

These people canned foods I'd never even heard of, and their gardens were right out in their front yards.

I looked at those kids as they walked down the road, and smelled the fresh air and the farmland and fields, and I said to Ron, "You could bury me here."

**I USED TO** have a recurring dream where I would die, and I'd be in a casket. And Ron was driving all over, towing this casket, because I couldn't figure out where to be buried. In California, there's no room to bury anyone anyway. When my grandfather died in 1950, he was buried in a drawer. I don't know why that was a big deal to me. But it was.

So, for me to say to Ron, "You could bury me here"—it was a really big deal.

After we got to Missouri, I never had that bad dream again.

We weren't at the farmhouse very long when I took a walk one morning with Ralph's wife, Kay, and she mentioned that she and Ralph had heard a story about some "bad Mormons."

I had heard that there were others in town who were nervous about "some Mormons" moving in. It always left me shaking my head and laughing at the way stories grow.

So I smiled and said, "You two are Baptist, right?"

She said, "Yes."

I said, "Are there any *bad* Baptists?"

"Well, sure there are," she said.

"Well, there's some bad Mormons too. We're people just like everybody else. There are good ones, and there are bad ones."

She nodded.

"Kay, you and Ralph don't ever have to worry about us," I told her. "We're good. We're all praying to the same God, trying to get into the same heaven."

"All right," she said, and that was that.

After we became really good friends, Ralph would sometimes say to me, "I just want you to convert and be a Baptist because I love you so much, and I don't want you to go to hell."

I'd laugh and say, "Ralph, we're just going to have to agree to disagree."

From time to time he would bring it up again, and I'd say, "If I go to hell, Ralph, I'm going to have had a good time doing it!"

I don't think God's going to send anyone to hell because they're a Baptist any more than He's going to send me to hell for being a Mormon. We're all children of God, and I think that becomes clearer when we get a chance to know one another as neighbors.


It wasn't long before Ralph invited me over to the main house to meet his sweet mother, Mildred. At the time, Mildred was in her late eighties, and right away when I sat down to talk, I noticed the gorgeous quilt she had on the sofa.

"Wow," I said. "This is really beautiful."

"Thank you," she said, and she showed me a few more she'd made too.

I was still sewing, making, fixing, stitching, all the time, but I hadn't really been interested in making quilts. As soon as I saw her quilts, though, I said, "Mildred, I really want to learn to quilt. Do you think you could teach me?"

"I would *love* to," she said.

"So what fabrics do I need?"

"Well, we just use old clothes and stuff. Scraps and pieces and that sort of thing," she said.

I always have a pretty big fabric stash, so I said, "I can probably come up with something like that. My sewing machine is kind of heavy, though. Do you want to do it at my house or yours?"

"Oh, honey, I don't use a sewing machine," she said. "I hand-stitch everything."

I thought about that for about a minute and then I looked at her and said, "You know what, Mildred, with all these kids I'm pretty sure that I'm not going to have the time to sit and sew things by hand, but thank you."

As much as I admired her handwork and the detail on those beautiful quilts, I knew that my brain didn't work that way. For *decades* I had been operating with only snippets of time to accomplish things, which is why I learned to do everything so quickly. My talent was in creating shortcuts—cooking shortcuts, sewing shortcuts, fixing shortcuts. Time may move much slower in Missouri, but that didn't mean that my brain could slow down yet.

Thankfully, Mildred wasn't offended. She hadn't had any neighbors for a very long time, so she was thrilled just to have the company.

I left there thinking about my own grandmother, who tried to teach me how to make Swedish meatballs. She would form one meatball with her hands. Then she would put it in a hot pan and cook it with oil while she patiently formed another meatball. Then she would take the first one out and put the next one in. She would stand near the stove looking at them, watching as she fried each one up individually. I can't imagine doing that! When I make Swedish meatballs, I take out a bread bowl that is as big around as my arms can reach. I pull out about five pounds of ground beef, add a whole bunch of seasonings at once, mix it together, and cook as many meatballs as I can fit onto a large cookie sheet, all at once.

I love Swedish meatballs! My kids love Swedish meatballs, but I cannot imagine spending all day making them.

Of course, my grandmother would be completely mortified that I make them the way I do, but it's the same meatball. It feeds my family. It serves its purpose.

# A Rural Education

As far as I was concerned, living and trying to survive at the farmhouse was the best education my kids could ever get. But shortly after we moved in, I called the local superintendent to talk about school.

I said, "I have these children who were homeschooled, and I'd like to enroll them in your school system." And he gave me a mouthful. He said, "Well, we're going to test them, and whatever grade they test at, we're putting them in that grade. I don't care if they're twelve years old and they test at a second-grade level, they're going to second grade."

"So if they test at twelfth grade," I asked him, "are you going to give them a diploma?"

In California, if you homeschooled your children it was generally because you wanted your kids to have a better education.

But according to this superintendent, in Missouri, if you home-schooled your kids it was usually because they were incorrigible, or because you needed their help on the farm.

So they tested my kids, and all of them—even the young ones—tested at well above their grade level.

I guess my homeschooling worked for us!

Rather than wait around for the school system to catch up to them, all three of my girls took their own unique paths. Natalie decided to get her GED right away. Sarah decided to go get a job. And Hillary decided to take a bus into town to go to high school. Two years later, she decided to test out and get her GED too. So all three of them completed their K–12 education ahead of their peers. That didn't mean they were finished learning. It just meant they felt free to set their sights on all the other parts of life a little early.

The boys were still a little young to do that, and they wanted to go to school as a way to make and keep friends in our new town. So we enrolled them in the K–8 school just a few miles up the road—a red-brick schoolhouse in the middle of farm country, with a small gym in the back. It held about thirty kids in the whole building.

Talk about stepping back in time.

The boys played basketball there, which was one of the first team sports they ever got involved in. And they made such close friends in that environment, it felt like they were gaining new siblings.

But the curriculum never kept up with the type of learning we had done at home.

One time, Jake turned in an assignment from his math book and told me, "Well, I did to page 40, but they made me erase back to page 11 so I wouldn't be ahead of everyone else."

We MAY HAVE BEEN A few years ahead when it came to school, but we still had so much to learn.

Right after our first Thanksgiving in Missouri, we all got excited about getting our Christmas tree. In California, we had a tradition of cutting down our tree the day after Thanksgiving, and we wanted to keep that tradition alive. But we had a hard time finding any real Christmas-tree farms around Hamilton. There just aren't that many pine trees in that part of the country, I guess, so people go out and cut their own little trees, which to me looked more like Christmas shrubs.

I asked Ralph if we could cut a tree from his property and he said, "You do not want to go the day after Thanksgiving."

"Well, that's our tradition. We always do that," I told him.

So he shrugged his shoulders and agreed to take us in his tractor with the flatbed. We climbed on the trailer and sang Christmas carols as we rode out on his property in search of a tree. We cut down a good family-sized tree, and we brought it home to decorate. And within five days, every single needle on that tree was on the floor.

We no longer had a Christmas tree. We had a Christmas stick!

The kids were so sad: "What happened to our tree?"

"Well, I tried to tell you," Ralph said. "Cedar trees don't keep their needles once they're cut."

We didn't want to wait until the night before Christmas to get ourselves a tree, so the next year we went out and bought a fake tree.

We sure made the most of that first Missouri Christmas, though.

Even though we weren't all together at home every day, I still wanted to do some activities as a family, like we did when we were homeschooling. So when I saw that the community theater in town was holding auditions for a Christmas musical, I signed

us up. And we all got in! To my delight, most of our kids partici-
pated. (And of course Ron was there to cheer us on from the
audience.) It was so much fun to get to meet and work and sing
together with so many local people.

One of the acts that joined in the show was a barbershop
quartet, and at one of the last rehearsals, just before our big
opening night, one of the quartet's members approached me.

"Are you Mrs. Doan?" he asked.

"Yes, I am," I said.

"Are you the same Mrs. Doan that used to homeschool her
children?"

I nodded and said, "Yes."

"Well," he said, and he looked me straight in the eyes, "I am
the school superintendent."

That's when it hit me that he was *the* superintendent.

"Mrs. Doan," he said, "I need to apologize to you. I'm so sorry
I treated you the way I did. Your family is really amazing."

We had a good laugh, and then I introduced him to each of
the kids.

The Christmas show was a blast.

I didn't know it then, but it would be a long time before all of
our kids would be together working on a creative project again.

--------

One day I uncovered a rock in our front-yard lawn. I decided to dig it up and move it out of the grass, but I dug
and dug until it was about three feet across, and I knew I wasn't
going to be able to lift it. So I called Ralph and asked him if he
could bring over his tractor and help me move that rock. We put
chains around it, and as he dragged it away we discovered a
hand-dug well. There was water in it. I tied a rock to a ball of

string and threw it to see how deep it was, and that well was seventy-five feet deep with forty feet of standing water. Ralph taught me and the kids about how they dug those wells back in the day, and then he looked at me and said, "Jenny, this water is worth more than gold. I suggest you just cover it back up and save it until you need it."

Ralph had memories of being on his farm right after the Dust Bowl, during the Great Depression, when the orchards died and every strawberry field in the area went dry. He said our two properties were the only places in the whole county where people could get water. People came from all over on wagons to fill up barrels of it.

Because his family and all of our neighbors' families had lived on this land for so long, they all drew from this giant well of knowledge, which I thought was just the coolest thing. Most of us move so fast, we never think about the long term.

These people recognized that life isn't always a continuous growing season.

After having moved so much, I thought it was really something that so many of these families had never moved in their lives. But when somebody *did* move, they held auctions to sell their things, and almost everything we needed for that farmhouse we were able to get at those auctions.

One time, Alan wanted a new bike so bad. He saved up five dollars over a couple of months, and when we heard there was an auction coming up, we took him with us. Lo and behold there were three nice bikes for sale that day. But the bids on those bikes started at five dollars.

Alan bid on each one, but the first two bikes sold for more than fifteen dollars apiece. He was so disappointed.

Well, the auctioneer noticed his disappointment, and on the third bike he said, "All right, starting it off at two dollars."

"I have five!" Alan shouted.

And the guy yelled, "Sold!"

"Yes!" Alan called out, pumping his big thirteen-year-old fists. He may have been tall, but even the auctioneer could see he was a kid at heart.

Ron and I looked at each other and smiled. There was so much humanity and kindness here.

We could count on one hand the times anyone came to visit, because we were "just so far away." Sometimes the mailman coming was a highlight of the kids' day. Randy Farmer was his name. He would drive his car down our road and come around that corner, then he'd speed up a little and hold the mail out his window, like a carrot, as the boys ran to see who could grab it.

Most families in the farm areas, they only had one or two kids. And it was such a long way between houses, we didn't see them very often. I was glad we had so many of us to keep each other company! But in town, there were half a dozen people who had bigger families than ours.

On Sundays, we would all pile into the van and go to church and see them all, and everyone was so friendly.

In truth, the farmhouse was only about a twenty-minute drive from town, but we still had that big old van. And big vans take a lot of gas. So, after Christmas was over, we could only make the trip to town maybe once a week—for grocery time or for church.

That forced us to plan in advance, just like our neighbors did, which was not unlike folks did in the olden days.

To save money, I would go up to the Amish stores, which we found out were located a little north of Hamilton, and we'd buy fifty-pound bags of potatoes, and fifty-pound bags of flour and sugar, real cheap, so we could make everything ourselves and rarely run out.

The fact that I already knew how to can was a blessing, because that made planning a whole lot easier. For example, I knew that we ate at least two tomato-based meals a week, spaghetti or tacos or something like that. We needed two quarts of tomatoes for those. So I had to can at least 104 quarts of tomatoes to make it through the year.

For milk? We had Ralph. He had kept one milking cow named Pam. A Jersey cow, which he said was better than Holstein cows, because Jersey cows gave the best milk ever. Josh or one of the other kids would help him milk Pam in the morning, and Ralph loved our family helping him. So he would bring us a gallon jar of milk twice a week. Instead of just drinking it, we would let it sit until the cream rose to the top, and then we would scoop that off. We put it in jars, and the kids shook it until it turned into butter or whipped cream. We had whipped cream on everything, because we didn't want the cream to go to waste. We had gotten used to drinking powdered milk in California, because real milk from the store was just so expensive. So this was a real treat.

For eggs? We got chickens. But not just any chickens. The boys got into Boy Scouts, and in the back of the Boy Scout magazine there were all these addresses where you could write to get catalogs for cool stuff. So Alan wrote to a specialty chicken farm, and they sent him a catalog, and the kids got together and ordered all these designer chickens in different colors. Some had fluffy heads, or fluffy feet, and they all laid different-color eggs.

They kept the chicks warm indoors as they raised them, and they named them after people we knew at church. "This is the Mr. Daniel chicken because he has really big hair," or "This one's Mrs. Wellington, 'cause she wears fancy shoes!"

We built a coop and we put some chicken wire around it. But we found out pretty quickly that chicken wire is no match for possums. The kids woke up one morning and found a bunch of broken eggs—and one dead chicken. They were heartbroken. We let them order a couple of new chickens, and they rigged up a homemade possum alarm: canning rings lined up on strings across the chicken wire, so if it jiggled at all, they would hear it and know something was getting into the coop.

The first time they heard that jingle, they popped out of bed and ran out to save their birds.

We owned a gun, a little .22 rifle, because everyone said we needed a gun on a property like ours. Now I knew why. I gave the gun to Alan and said, "Go take care of those chickens!" Alan went outside and a few minutes later he came running back into the house. "I can't do it! I can't do the killing thing," he said. "I can't."

I understood. I couldn't have shot a possum, either.

"All right. You bring the light, Jake. And bring the cage. We'll go catch this possum instead."

Now, possums are diggers, so this possum was digging down when I grabbed ahold of his tail and started pulling. I'm a strong woman, and I pulled with all my strength. But he wasn't budging. Then all of a sudden he let loose! My arm swung back, and this possum went flying through the air.

"Open that cage!" I shouted.

The possum flew through the sky and somehow landed smack in the middle of the cage. Jake closed the door and we all stood there excited, and terrified. For some reason we all started laughing hysterically. Once I caught my breath, Alan carefully put that cage in the car, and we drove a few miles down the road and let him go.

Of course he came right back the very next night.

That's when we sent Ron out to shoot him.

Ron's the kind of guy that when a bird flies into the machine shop, he'll spend half the afternoon trying to catch it or shoo it out safely so it doesn't get hurt. But we couldn't let the possum keep killing our chickens. We needed those eggs! So he went out, and he pointed that gun right between its eyes, and he pulled the trigger—and it didn't work. The bullet bounced right off its head and the thing just ran away!

It turns out a possum's skull is stronger than a .22-caliber bullet. How could we have known that? Ralph then taught us that the only way to kill a possum is to shoot it behind the ears. So the next time that possum came back, that's where Ron shot him. But it wasn't a clean shot, and that poor animal suffered before it died. Ron was heartbroken.

The next morning, the kids dug some stronger fencing deeper into the ground. They fortified that chicken coop like a little fortress so we wouldn't have to kill any more possums after that. But it wasn't the only animal encounter we had in those first few months at the farmhouse.

Another day, Jake came running in: "Mom, you've got to help us. Bring a weapon!"

I was mopping, so I ran out with my mop in hand, ready to fight, only to find the boys up in a tree fort looking down at a badger.

"Boys," I said. "A badger can bite through a car tire. Move your fort. Leave it alone. This mom is not going to help you fight a badger!"

Another night, I was driving home in the thickest fog I'd ever seen when this giant animal walked up out of a ditch right in front of my car. Most people hit deer in the road, but not me. I hit a cow. It didn't do any damage to the cow, because I was creeping along so slowly. But in Missouri, if you hit a cow, the farmer is liable because that cow isn't supposed to be out on the public road. Well, the cow's owner heard the commotion and he came right out and said, "I don't know whose cow this is, but I'll put him in my pasture until somebody claims him."

I laughed and said, "Really? Because he's got a yellow tag on his ear like all the rest of your cows!"

Another time when Josh and I were driving to the farmhouse, I spotted a deer in the middle of the road and slammed on the brakes. Usually a deer will run away pretty fast, but this deer just stood there. She didn't even flinch.

"What is going on with that deer?" I said to Josh.

We both looked at it, expecting it would move but it didn't, so I said, "Josh, get out of the car and go shush that deer off the road."

Josh got out and waved his hands at it saying, "Shush!"

But that deer still did not move. It was *weird*.

So Josh walked right up to it and started petting it like a dog.

When it still didn't move, he reached down and picked up one of its front paws and waved at me with the deer's hoof!

"I don't know what's the matter with her, Mom. I think she might be in shock or something," he said.

We didn't know what else to do, so he kind of picked her front legs up and moved her a few steps, and then pushed her back legs and walked her off to the side of road.

I wish I could have caught it on video. I think we would have won the $10,000 prize on one of those TV shows.


WE JUST KEPT RUNNING INTO things (literally!) that you would never know you didn't know 'til you lived way out in the country. But as I predicted, Ralph helped us to learn everything we ever needed to know. And having those connections to the past and more than two hundred acres of land to explore, the children made some of their best memories ever.

So many Boy Scout campouts were held on the land around the farmhouse. The kids played paintball. They built elaborate forts all up in the trees.

Ron spent hours and hours teaching them all to ride motor-cycles, and every ride was on that land, on trails they cleared and jumps they built with their own bare hands.

We even picked up a trampoline at an auction, and the kids were free to run out and jump on it in their underwear if they wanted—because there was nobody around.

I can still hear those squeals of laughter. The six of them all playing together.

Our kids had such a grand childhood, and our summers seemed to last forever.

But isn't it funny how fast the years go?

# Six Quilts &
# a Forever Home

At home, whether it was in California, Oregon, or Missouri, I was always sewing. With so many kids, somebody always needed something, and I couldn't afford to run out and buy things. I'd sew at the dining room table while keeping an eye on the kids. I'd get up early in the morning and sew, and I'd sit down late at night and sew. But it was also something I did to unwind from the day. It's where I found my peace. It's still where I find peace. Some people get peace from running. Some people like to clean or read. I get my peace from sewing.

My grandmother used to say to me: "It's a sin to sew on Sunday. If you sew on a Sunday you're going to have to pick it out with your nose on Monday!" But I chose to leave that advice behind, along with her way of cooking meatballs, because Sundays turned into my favorite day to sew. On Sundays, Ron was home, so the day was much more relaxing. I could sew without having to keep watch at the same time.

During our first spring in the farmhouse, I found myself working steadily on a dress for Hillary's high school choir concert. Hillary worked on it too. And usually she would grab whatever I made and dash off excited to try it on, but this time she stopped, looked at me, and said, quietly, "I just realized that if you didn't know how to sew, I probably wouldn't have had these gowns, because we couldn't afford them, could we?"

"No, we could not afford them," I said.

"But you were able to make these beautiful dresses for us," she said, "and to teach me how to sew too."

She smiled and walked over and gave me the biggest hug.

SINCE THE THEATER DIDN'T NEED me as a costumer, and the kids were too big to wear matching clothing anymore, I was really at a loss for something creative to do with my sewing.

So I finally decided to sign up for a quilting class at the vo-tech over in Chillicothe.

My first class was making a "Log Cabin" quilt. I had no idea what that meant, but I was willing to give it a try

One night a week, I drove to the school to join a group of the kindest, most loving women who would gather together to learn about quilting. Having pieced things together all my life, I took to it right away. And I loved it! I quickly came up with some shortcuts, which allowed me to cut patterns and put together squares in sets instead of one at a time, and by the end of the eight-week class, instead of making one quilt, I had made six.

Making those quilts was hands down the most creative thing I'd ever done.

In that class we also learned a bit about the value of quilts, of old quilts that had been found in antique stores or passed down for generations in families. I thought about the beautiful quilts Mildred made, and the quilt my mother took the time to make for me, and I realized that these quilts I made might outlive me by generations. And for me, that realization—the longevity of it—was such a wonderful realization.

I had sewn lots of clothing, but the kids were constantly outgrowing whatever I made. The styles changed, or the season changed. If I made a costume, somebody used it one time; it would look good from twenty feet out and hold together for two weeks.

Quilting had a much more intimate feel than making costumes or clothes. The whole idea of it, of making something that people would hold, and use, maybe treasure, and hopefully wrap themselves up in, gave me so much joy. And the timing of my newfound hobby couldn't have been better, because I would soon have a reason to make a very special quilt for a very special little baby boy.

IT WAS ABOUT A YEAR after moving to Missouri when Natalie met a man and she told me she wanted to get married. I tried to give her as much wisdom from my own experiences as I could, but she was determined. I had to pick my battles. And it wasn't long before she got married, moved out, and after a few months we were surprised and excited to learn that she was pregnant with my first precious grandson.

The next year marked my fortieth birthday, and Sarah put signs up and down the gravel road to the farmhouse that said, "Lordy, Lordy, Mama's 40! Honk for her birthday!" Very few people ever drove down our road, so it seemed silly, until Ralph got into his car (with 11,000 miles on it) and drove up and down the road honking his horn.

We were having our usual birthday with homemade cake when Ralph came over again carrying a five-foot wild hemp plant. He left it on the porch with a note attached that said, "If anybody needs this, it's you." We all laughed so hard.

I had a lot more to celebrate—and to sew—soon after, because within a couple of years Sarah met a wonderful man named Seth, and they got married, and then Hillary surprised us with an engagement announcement that same year too.

After making the first two girls' dresses, I was on the lookout for fabric for Hillary even before she told us her happy news. So, when the time came, we made the most beautiful embossed white brocade wedding dress ever, using an entire roll of the most gorgeous fabric that I found at a thrift store for a dollar a yard.

Before long, I was blessed to be a grandma to three precious little souls. And as each one of my daughters greeted their first-born babies, we wrapped them up in the love and care that went into their own handmade quilts. It didn't matter to me if they'd drag it around on the ground or if they got it all dirty. I'd be happy if they held onto it until they were ready to go to college, when they might say, "I need a new quilt, because Winnie the Pooh can't come with me."

That's when I realized that I'm a certain kind of quilter: a utilitarian quilter.

There are all sorts of quilters in the world. Modern quilters, art quilters. And they do such beautiful work. But I've never made things to sit on the shelf or hang on a wall. I want them to be loved, used, and worn out.

———

Five years and one day after moving to the farmhouse, we got another surprise. A young woman, a realtor from town, called me out of the blue. She said, "Mrs. Doan, this is going to sound really weird to you, but a guy has put a house up for sale and I had a feeling to call you."

"You had a feeling?" I said.

"I know," she said, "that must sound so weird to you, and I've never done anything like this before. I'm sorry if I'm bothering you."

"No, no." I said. "If you had a feeling to call me, I am interested in that."

So I let her tell me a little bit about this random house in Hamilton. We weren't even thinking about moving again, but I said I would take a look the next time we got over to town.

When I drove up to the house, the first thing I noticed was that it was a complete and total mess. There was no front porch where there was supposed to be a porch. The siding was falling off. The roof was in rough shape. It had plywood on the back.

When I walked inside, I saw the same. There was no floor in the living room, just joists, and there was more plaster fallen on the floor than there was on the walls. But then I saw these two, large, beautiful carved-wood pillars in the entryway, and what was left of the rare old Victorian details, and it took my breath away. I couldn't stop imagining what that house could be. Where other people saw an old tear-down, I saw the possibilities. I knew what some love and time and care could turn that house into.

That night, I could hardly sleep. I told Ron about it, and I told him I thought we should buy it. "I have a feeling we're going to need to move," I said.

Then, out of the blue, we got a call from Courtney Diddle.

"I'm sorry, Jenny," he said, "but I'm going to have to start charging you rent."

"Well, Courtney," I said, "you know what we put into this house here, and with that investment we should be able to live here for about another thirteen years."

He said, "I know. And I'm so sorry, but I have to go into a nursing home. And I have to be able to pay for the nursing home, so I need the income."

Naturally we talked about buying the farmhouse, and we had saved for a long time, but Courtney wasn't interested in selling to us. "It's our family home," he said.

When I got off the phone, I looked over at Ron and said, "Well, we've got our answer."

Ron and I started looking forward to finally becoming the owners of our own home again, and we knew the bottom line: if we didn't like it, or it didn't work out, we would be okay— because we had each other.

It was not so easy for the boys, especially Josh, because he truly loved the farming life. And when Ralph found out? He was furious.

He wasn't *really* furious. He was just so hurt that Courtney wouldn't sell us the farm. When we left, it was so hard, because we knew it about broke his heart.

———

The house in Hamilton was listed for $25,000, and nobody thought it was worth that much. Everyone in town thought it should be torn down because it was such an eyesore.

The family that owned it had apparently wanted to fix it up, but they got low on funds, so for some time they had been selling off parts of it just to make ends meet. That's where the doors and windows in the back had gone, and why there was no floor or cabinets in the kitchen, and no front porch. That kind of resourcefulness to make ends meet was familiar to me. So when the realtor said to me, "Mrs. Doan, you need to make an offer, because it is *not* worth $25,000," I said, "Nope."

I knew it was a Mission Victorian built in the 1800s, which meant it had good bones and it was built to last. Which meant it would be worth quite a bit more than $25,000 the moment Ron and I got our hands on it. I also knew we had saved enough to make a small down payment, so affording the mortgage wouldn't be a problem.

People had always stepped up and helped us when we struggled in the past. And I had my mother in my mind again, whispering, "When you cast your bread . . . it comes back buttered." So I said to the realtor, "I'm going to pay what they are asking."

There were houses all around this old house, and most of our new neighbors had moved into those houses in the '50s and '60s. They had raised their families in those houses, and they were older now and lived pretty quiet lives before we came to town with our teenagers. So, as soon as we moved in, we baked cookies and took them over to introduce ourselves, which seemed to be something that hadn't happened for them in a long time.

We had done the same thing whenever we moved to a new place in California, too, but there it felt like people wore busy like a badge. Maybe I did, too, at the time, but not in Hamilton. In Hamilton, people had lots of time for cookies, and conversations, and fun. Everywhere we went, people would ask, "Well, Mrs. Doan, how's that house coming?" Or they would comment, "Oh, we haven't been in that house since we were children. It's so good to see it getting fixed up."

We didn't have much of a fix-it-up budget, but we worked together to get things done. The boys and I shoveled several dumpster loads of old plaster out of the house, and pulled the old lath (the wooden slats) out of the walls so we could put up sheet rock. And then one afternoon, Ron came home and was shocked to see the oak floor in the living room was completely put back together.

"Wow, Jenny. How did you do that?" he asked.

"Well," I said, "I discovered that the lath that was on the walls is oak, and it's the same size as the skinny oak boards on the floors. So I started nailing it down on the floor!"

He smiled and laughed, and for the rest of the first week we sanded and finished it together. It came out looking just as nice as the original oak floors in the rest of the house, at basically no cost! It's hard to describe the satisfaction that came with finishing that house, knowing that we wouldn't have to move again; knowing that this was where our grown children and grandchildren would gather around the table, in this home that would be our forever home.

We weren't there long when I noticed one of our neighbors had cut up a tree, so I went over and asked them if they would consider dumping the chip pile in my yard so I could use it for mulch. They were more than happy just to get it off their lawn! It was a huge mound that not only saved us money, but when Jacob saw it he got all excited. He grabbed a piece of plywood that we had pulled off of the back of the house and he set it on the mound and started jumping his dirt bike over it. That's when another neighbor from across the street walked slowly over to talk to me with a twinkle in his eye and said, "Every morning, I get in my chair and I just sit right there by the window, because I know something's going to happen at this house!"

Just like at the farmhouse, our neighbors seemed to appreciate the company of our big family full of fun and energy.

When most of the work fixing up the main floor of the house was finished, we invited all of our neighbors to an open-house party. We made all sorts of treats for everyone to eat, and one of our neighbors, a man nearly ninety years old, climbed the stairs to the new front porch and slowly shuffled into the living room. He sat down, opened up his old banjo case, and started plucking the strings with the speed and precision of a much younger man. He played some old songs that everyone recognized, and I started singing, and a whole bunch of our guests joined in. That music and all of our neighbors filled our home with so much love.

---

B efore moving to Missouri and out to the farmhouse, we never would have imagined that we'd make memories involving chickens and possums and cows and hand-dug wells. And now, we were making memories and sharing beautiful experiences that we couldn't have imagined before moving into town.

One of my favorite days in Hamilton is an annual tradition called Drive Your Tractor to School Day. And it's exactly what the name says: it's a day when all the kids drive their tractors to school in a parade right down the middle of the main street. Some of the tractors cost more than the homes these families live in. They're beasts! You could drive a car under the center of them. But these kids handle them fine because they've been driving them since they were old enough to reach the controls. If they don't have a tractor, they drive a lawnmower. The townspeople all come out of their homes and businesses to watch the children from the sidewalk. They cheer and take pictures. It seems like something out of a Norman Rockwell painting.

So do Fridays in the fall, when we listen for the clip-clop of horses on the street, which lets us know the Amish wagons are arriving. Those wagons are full of bright-colored mums and pumpkins and yummy homemade baked pies that they sell on the honor system in the center of our little town.

Somehow the fact that we'd made our forever home in such a wonderful, slow-paced town seemed to drive home just how quickly time was flying.

Our kids weren't little anymore. Any of them. One by one, they were growing up and moving out so fast I could hardly believe it.

When you try to explain how time flies to new mothers, they rarely understand it. They have no idea what those words mean until it happens to them. It's one of those things. One day you are barely getting through, hanging on by the skin of your teeth, and the exhausting hours are filled to the top with the endless to-do lists and the ceaseless, ever-changing needs of a busy family. Time is filled with laughter and messes and hugs and teaching and fixing broken bones, or mending broken hearts. And then suddenly you find yourself alone in a quiet, clean house. And the hours slow down like a turtle crawling across a road. And you wonder, "What happened?"

You wonder, "What *now*?"

14

# What About the Next Fifty Years?

What does a full-time, stay-at-home, homeschooling mom do when she suddenly finds she has time on her hands? Time—the one thing there never seemed to be enough of?

I certainly wasn't content keeping house or spending time alone. So as soon as Josh was launched, I took a job.

There was a chiropractor in town, who liked being a chiropractor, but his true passion was baking pies. So, in his seventies, he decided to follow that passion and opened up a little restaurant called the Filling Station. My first job while trying to find fulfillment as an empty nester was working at the Filling Station.

The restaurant sat about a dozen people, and in a small town with hardly any restaurants for miles, we ended up having quite a few regulars who would come in every day. They would open the door and hear me singing or whistling away. I didn't love cooking, but I did love to have fun. So I looked at the job of slinging hamburgers and making eggs as an excuse to have fun with the customers.

"I want some eggs, Jenny. And make 'em hard!" one customer said every time he came in. After hearing that request about a dozen times, I went out and bought a couple of plastic toy eggs and put them on his plate and took them out to him.

"This hard enough for you?"

Oh did we laugh. It was really so much fun, but that chiropractor-who-loved-to-bake-pies couldn't make the twelve-seat restaurant business work in our little town. He ended up closing shop.

When that ended, I took another job as a cook, this time over at the nursing home. I went in whistling and singing, ready for fun. So, when a resident said he didn't like onions, one day at lunch I sent his plate out under a covered metal dome, like usual. But when the orderly placed it in front of him and lifted the dome, the only thing on the plate was a whole raw onion.

He laughed so hard! But aside from the laughter, I wasn't sure cooking was for me. They eventually got a new cook, and I decided to try something new.

Before taking another job, I slowed down for a minute and put some thought into what made me really happy.

I was really happy being a mom. I was happy homeschooling. I loved working together, building our homes and our family. And I was happiest when I was able to make a difference. And no matter what I did, I realized that the thing I always wanted, or *needed*, was to be able to have fun.

That's when I saw a posting for a teacher's aide position at a local school. I thought maybe I could apply a lot of what made me really happy at that school. So I put in an application—and

I got the job! But this wasn't a regular school. It was an alternative school. And these weren't your average kids. They were children who were considered *incorrigible*. Some had come from homes where the parents couldn't handle them. Some didn't have parents at all. A lot of them had been in some type of trouble with their regular schools, and quite a few of them had been in trouble with the law.

Some of them wore ankle bracelets.

None of that bothered me. I have always felt that if people could just be loved, if they could just be listened to, then it would make all the difference in the world. I still believe that. I walked into that school with my guitar and my books feeling hopeful and ready to do some loving on those challenged, lost, and ornery kids.

Working with children was usually a breeze for me. I'm usually everybody's favorite mama. But for these kids, I knew I needed to walk in armed with a plan. My first matter of business was reading. I knew reading would change the world for them, just like it did for my own kids, but since many of them couldn't read, I told them I was going to read to them.

"We're not listening to any blippity-bleep book!" they said.

"That's fine," I responded. "You don't have to listen. I'm just going to read to you anyway."

So, after lunch, I sat down and started reading out loud. They mostly sulked or stood against the walls looking uninterested and trying hard to ignore me. Then, when I got to a really good part, I closed up the book, and said, "Well, that's all for today."

I moved on to other lessons, and the next day, I did it again. I stopped at a really, really good part. Only this time when I closed the book and stood up, more than one of those kids pleaded, "No! Don't stop. You can't stop!"

I stopped anyway.

By the third day, I had a big kid sitting on each side of my chair and another one sitting at my feet as I read. And when I went home that night I felt like maybe, just *maybe* I had found my purpose.

DAY BY DAY, I WORKED with those kids, and I always tried to make it fun by reading and singing. When they were stressed out and short-tempered and angry, which they were a lot, they would get into fights. It's all they knew how to do. So I stepped in and broke up those fights and I'd say, "You go to that corner and you, over there."

When they wanted to swear, I'd say, "Okay. You want to swear? You can swear. But you have to make up your own swear words." Before long they learned to stop and catch themselves, and say something like "What the marshmallow."

In addition to reading to them, I sang to them. After a few weeks of singing, mostly by myself, a big, older boy, who was probably six foot four—so, taller than me—chested right up to me. I braced myself, unsure of his intention, but then he looked down at me and asked, softly, "Could you just sing 'Puff the Magic Dragon' one more time?"

"Sure I can!" I said. And I whipped out my guitar.

After that, when a fight broke out that I couldn't stop, some of the stronger boys stepped in front of me to protect me. I went from having their backs turned to me and being one more person in their lives that they hated on, to being someone they protected and cared about.

Little by little, more than a few of those kids became less guarded. They started to trust me. Some of them even started to learn. And more important: they started to *laugh*.

It didn't take long before I got to know some of the kids in my classroom really well, and there was one boy in particular who could barely read. He lived about forty-five minutes away, and there was no one to drive him to school and back. The school director ended up buying a car we could use to shuttle some of these kids where they needed to go, so I offered to get him to school and take him back home.

Until we met, this boy had never heard of knock-knock jokes. So, every night on the drive to his home, I would say, "Knock, knock."

And he'd say, "Who's there?" and I'd respond with just the silliest, simplest answers.

"Boo!"

"Boo who?"

"Awww, why are you crying?" I'd say, and he'd take a second and then laugh so much.

He especially loved the potty humor.

"Knock-knock?"

"Who's there?"

"Europe."

"Europe who?"

"No, *you're* a poo!"

I'd tell another and another and we'd laugh so much our sides hurt.

After a while, I started printing out knock-knock jokes from the internet. I handed them to him and said, "Here. Here's some more. Read these to me, since I'm driving."

All the way home I had him practicing reading, and he didn't even realize it.

But when we got to his house, that laughter would change abruptly.

"Can you stay? Can you please stay longer?" he would ask.

Like so many of his classmates, this boy just had nothing at all to go home to.

For a while, Ron, who had always been supportive of me no matter what I did, got worried that I might try to adopt them all.

I spent my time loving on these kids, giving them my heart, and I knew it really mattered. But I would learn the hard way that sometimes, no matter how hard you try, no matter how many hours you spend, some of them just don't have a chance.

Over and over my heart got shredded, and I carried my tears home with me every night.

Ron and our own kids had been worried about me for a while when Alan and Sarah happened to come over one night, after yet another tragedy involving one of those kids. They were both in a great mood, talking and sharing details about some really good things that were happening in their own lives, but I could hardly hear a word they said.

I was drowning in sadness.

One of them, I don't even remember who, came over and gave me a great big hug, which I probably really needed, and then they both insisted, "Mom, we have got to find something else for you to do. You cannot keep doing this. Our happy mom is so sad."

I had gone from being this really joyful person—and I *am* joyful, it's in my very nature—to being deeply sad and heart-broken.

It was my turn to listen now, and to learn from my kids.

It broke my heart, but I had to leave that job. I cared about each and every one of those kids, but my children were right. It was killing me.

A few months after I left the school, the kids were over and we were at the table and the conversation turned to what I should do next. Everyone had an option or an idea for me but *me*. I rejected everything they suggested.

So Alan turned and asked me directly, "Mom, what do you want to *do* for the next fifty years of your life?"

*Fifty years.*

It struck me so hard: if I lived to the age of my grandmother, I had more life ahead of me than I had behind me.

Being a full-time mom had been so meaningful. So *important.* What could possibly be as important or fulfilling as that?

"Alan," I said. "I don't know."

———

While I was busy trying to find my new purpose in life, all the kids had been well on their way to creating their own lives for some time. By 2008, Natalie had five children and was living in Cameron, about fifteen minutes away. Sarah and her husband, Seth, an electrical foreman who worked in Kansas City, had five kids, too, having just adopted a son from a girl that we knew when our own kids were growing up in California. They lived in Kidder, about five minutes away.

Hillary and her husband, Alex, had moved to Amarillo, Texas, with four little girls between the ages of one and eight, and a little baby boy on the way. Jake had married Misty, his high school sweetheart, after returning from a mission to Indianapolis, Indiana (just like Ron!). They had two kids and were living in Kearney, about forty minutes away. And Josh was doing marketing for a website and living in Salt Lake City, Utah, with his wife, Amanda.

Which leaves Alan. Alan started working for a major company almost as soon as he turned eighteen, and it wasn't a surprise that he was promoted right away. But when he was called to go on a mission for our church, he set his professional life aside for two years. God called him to Ukraine, where he made some great friends and gained so much experience that when he came home, he got another good job at another big company right away. But a few months into it, he came to us and said, "I've got to go college. Everybody who I work with has a degree. They will respect me more if I have the paper."

Without studying, he went and took the ACT and did his first two semesters at Missouri Western State College (now University) in St. Joseph. Alan being Alan, he figured if he was going to finish school "for real," he might as well go get his degree in Hawaii instead of Missouri. So he applied to Brigham Young University Hawaii as a transfer student, with a 4.0 average. (Which was much more attractive to a university than a home-school kid with a GED.) We tried to get government assistance with his tuition, but between Ron's work and my jobs, we made $2,000 too much in income to qualify for federal help, which made no sense at all. How could $2,000 be the difference between getting some help and getting no help at all, when that wasn't nearly enough to cover tuition? The system made no sense to me.

Fortunately for him, Alan grew up learning how to make do, how to fix anything, how to be resourceful, and how to have fun while he did it. And he was so technically advanced for his age that he basically ended up running the computers for the university's information systems department, where he was majoring. His professors all loved him, but Alan was so poor he could barely eat. So he found jobs and juggled school and somehow managed to scrape together enough money to pay for Ron and me to come to his graduation—in Hawaii! It was so beautiful, and we had so much fun.

Almost all of our other kids got married right away. But not Alan. He basically spent a decade being an entrepreneur while couch surfing.

He was home between jobs and hanging out with me when one day I randomly said to him, "Alan, I'm going out to pick up a quilt."

"What quilt?" he asked.

"I don't remember," I said. "I dropped it off at the long-armers a year ago."

A long-arm quilting machine is like a giant sewing machine with a big, long arm over a quilt-sized table. It's designed to complete the final step in the quilt-making process. It reaches out over the whole quilt when it's laid out flat, and it does the stitching that holds the three layers of the quilt together — the top, the back, and the batting that gets sandwiched in the middle. People who don't want to hand-stitch their quilts send their pieced-together quilts to a long-armer, who has one of these machines. They do the stitching over the whole quilt in patterns of flowers or circles, or whatever pattern you choose.

"Wait, it takes a whole year to stitch one quilt?" Alan asked.

"No, no. I'm guessing it only takes half a day. But the long-arm quilter I use is all backed up. Most long-armers won't even take new quilts until they clear their backlog."

"Mom, that means there's a lot of demand for this," he said. "Could you do this? Could you run one of those machines?"

"I don't know," I said. "I'm getting older. I don't know if I could learn a whole new thing."

But Alan was hooked. He talked to Sarah about it, and for the next week they did the research and discovered that the machines can cost tens of thousands of dollars. Still, the demand for this service was definitely high, he said, which told him that it could be profitable. The more information he dug up, the more excited he got, and he kept talking to me about it, but I really wasn't that interested.

I finally said, "Alan, here's what you have to realize. Quilting is a *hobby*. This would just be filling up my time. I am not okay with filling up my time for the next fifty years. I need to do something that *matters*."

# A (Missouri) Star Is Born

It was right around this time that the stock market crashed. Ron and I lost most of our retirement savings overnight. It wasn't much. Just what we had in a 401(k). Even so, 2008 was the first time our kids had ever witnessed a major downturn in their adult lives, and they were worried about us.

Their worry wasn't helped any when we mentioned that Ron's job might be in jeopardy. Ron had landed a good job as a machinist at the *Kansas City Star*, working on their massive printing presses A lot of other newspapers in the country had switched to a digital-only model, and everyone's job security was shaken that year. But our kids weren't raised to sit around and worry. They were raised to do something about it, whatever *it* was. And in this case, Alan decided to double down on his plan to turn me into a long-arm quilter.

Part of his confidence that he could turn this extension of my hobby into something profitable came from watching his younger brother Jake in action.

Jake had been out of high school for a while and, like me, he'd been trying to figure out what he wanted to do. After marrying his wife, Misty, and seeing all of the planning and money that went into a wedding, he decided to create a start-up company offering services and setup for weddings and events. He didn't have any training in it, but since he grew up figuring things out, he figured everything out from scratch, which made him our family's first entrepreneur.

Whether he knew how to do something or not, anything a customer asked for, Jake's answer was always, "Yes, we can do that."

It was only after he said yes that he'd try to figure it out, or call me or Alan or one of his other siblings and say, "Help! How do we do this?"

Where Alan was good with working things out in his mind, and working things out on computers, Jake was especially gifted with his hands. He could build or create *anything*. So he learned how to set up rented lighting and tents and tables, and build stages, and create any sort of decorations or themes a bride and groom envisioned. And when a bride had a special request for colored tablecloths, he would order up giant rolls of fabric. Next thing I knew, a semitruck full of satin would pull up and unload at my house.

I'd have to call him up and say, "Jake, do you want to tell me about this?"

"Yeah! Mom, we need thirty-six round tableclothes by Tuesday. Go!"

No questions asked, I was sewing tablecloths. And that's how we did things in our family. I raised them to work together, so that's what they knew how to do.

Without even knowing it, Jake lit the entrepreneurial spark in Alan, who was quietly on the sidelines learning and watching Jake the whole time. It was Alan who would come up with his own ideas for the quilting business, and then combine that idea with his college and consulting experiences to create what would eventually become our company.

Alan ran the numbers and figured out that to make the payment on the loan for a long-arm quilting machine I'd only have to do about four quilts a week. And if I could do two in a day, that would mean sixty quilts a month! If I could bring in that much business, that meant we would be able to pay for the loan, the thread, the supplies, the electricity, and then there would be a little steady income for me and Ron to build a nest egg and maybe even a little profit from what was left over. And since all the long-armers were backed up, and there was a long waiting list for the service, we were hopeful that there would be a steady demand.

To Alan, who was always good with numbers and with business, the economics made good sense. And the bottom line was, if it didn't work out, we would be fine, because no matter what we would still have each other.

I still wasn't in love with the whole idea, but I did love my kids—and making them happy always made me happy. So if Alan thought it was a really good investment, I knew enough to listen to that.

Alan scraped together some cash, and together with Sarah and her husband, Seth, they decided to go in together to buy me a quilt machine. But then they found out that there was no way it was going to fit in our house! The machine was too big to get through any door we had, which meant they were going to have to buy a building just to put that machine in.

Lucky for us, Hamilton was full of old empty commercial buildings in the downtown area. They found an old auto mechanic's building with plenty of room for the machine in the former repair bay, with an office space in the front that would work well for a counter where I could greet customers. There was even a big storage area in the back, in case we ever needed it. And it was cheap, as far as commercial buildings go. But the only way they could come up with the money to buy it was for Sarah and Seth to take out a second mortgage on their house.

After running the numbers and talking it over with Alan, they decided to go for it.

> **ALAN:** If a younger me approached me with this idea today and said, "I think I can do this," I'd probably tell him, "This is a bad business, man. Do *not* do this." We had to do five quilts a week just to break even, and when we opened the doors of the shop, we did not get close to that. And even if we did get over twenty a month, it would be a little "service business" to make a little money on the side. So I would not have recommended taking a second mortgage on a house to do this.
>
> I would say, "You should save up some cash, and if you still want to, go buy a cute little quilt machine for Grandma. It's going to be fine." Because now, it feels very risky to me, because a huge part of this business was not built on the internet. It was built in the personal relationships made in a very small shop in a very small town, where you have to really think: *Is this a great idea to mortgage a house and to put sixty grand at risk for this?*
>
> But at the time, Sarah and I were only thinking, *We'll do this for Mom.*
>
> We were thinking about all of the reasons we would succeed, and none of the reasons we might fail.

The whole family came together to get that shop up and running. We scraped wallpaper and knocked down walls. We raised a new wall between the shop and the old garage space. Ron built some shelves. We threw some paint on the walls of the space in the front and fixed up the counter a little bit, to make it look cute. I put a couple of bolts of fabric on the new shelves behind the counter, so it looked like a place where quilts might get made, and we opened the doors for business that fall of 2008.

The Missouri Star Quilt Company was born!

Setting up a shop outside of our home made it feel more like a business than a hobby to me, and that was probably a good thing. I felt like I had work to do, a job to go to, and I wanted to do it well so Sarah and Alan didn't feel like they'd made a mistake.

When the machine arrived, right away I learned that it didn't matter how fast *I* worked, the machine could only go so fast. I couldn't control any part of that. I had to stay up really late and get up really early to keep it going.

I had been a piecer for my whole life, so at any given moment I had an entire bin full of materials—the "pieces pile"—that I made into tops that were ready to be quilted. So I practiced on my own quilts. And when I ran out, I practiced on all my friends' quilts, and all of a sudden, I was quilting.

But nobody came. Sometimes a week would go by and we wouldn't get any customers. We did take out one or two ads in the newspaper, but that was all we could afford, because we didn't have any money in the budget for advertising. But we did have friends, neighbors, and family come in. Mostly they came in to talk, which was just fine with me, because I love to talk!

But then they started asking me questions about quilts, and quilting.

They asked me things like, "How do I get this spot out?" or "How do I hang this?" or, "How should I fold this?" The only knowledge I had was my own experience, so that's what I shared with them. And, to my surprise, I was able to answer just about any question they had.

Then one neighbor came in with her great-grandma's quilt. The fabric was so old it was falling apart, and she wanted to find a way to save it.

I looked it over and held this beautiful old quilt in my hands, and I said, "All right, here's the deal. Do you want to keep this in a box? Or do you want to actually have this out so you can use it?"

"I'd like to be able to use it," she answered.

I suggested we lay a piece of netting over it to hold all the fabric together and then we could quilt over the top of it and that would preserve it for another period of time. I'm certain it was not the historically correct thing to do, and it was not what a museum would tell her to do, but a quilt specialist at a museum would tell her, "Don't use it!"

I didn't follow rules. I didn't have any special training or traditional quilting background. I didn't even know there *were* rules. I would just figure it out, whatever it was.

When the work on her quilt was finished, our neighbor was thrilled. She was so happy that she could use her great-grandmother's quilt again. Seeing her smile and hold it and touch it to her face was more than enough payment for all the work I'd done to save it. I almost let her go without charging her! If it weren't for the loans from Alan and Sarah, I most likely would have done that.

IT WAS NOT LONG AFTER opening that I realized there had been a deep passion in the quilting world for many years, maybe decades or even centuries, to make quilting seem really, really hard. The general feeling in the quilting world was that everything had to be *perfect*, which made it so difficult it was almost unattainable. If your stitches weren't straight or your corners weren't aligned, or your designs weren't symmetrical, some old-school teachers would make you rip out the stitches and do it again. I met a whole lot of neighbors and friends and the occasional walk-in customer who carried around the feeling of, "I can't do this. It's not my thing."

*But they* could *do it,* I thought. It was only that their desire had been beaten dead by the old rules and old ways of doing things.

And that was not me.

After the kids grew up, since I had more time on my hands, I made so many quilts that I never could have afforded to have them all machine-quilted. Even if I could, the long-armers were too backed up. So I had taken to hand-quilting—as Ralph's mother, Mildred, had done with her quilts back when we lived out at the farmhouse. There was one big difference, though: my hand-stitching was anything but amazing. I mean, a beginner could have done as good a job as I did, because I wasn't worried about it being perfect. I was worried about getting it done quickly, and making sure it held together, because it was going on a bed to keep somebody warm or going into the hands of a child so they could drag it around with them wherever they went.

All I wanted for my quilts was for them to be loved and used. And as a few more people started trickling into the shop to see what I was up to, I realized that a lot of them found it interesting, and freeing in a way, when I told them I was a utilitarian quilter and explained to them what that meant to me.

To help break down the old, intimidating way of doing things even more, I compiled examples of all of the little quick tricks and shortcuts I had come up with over the years. So when someone said, "Oh, I can't make a quilt. It's too complicated," I would say, "Can I just show you something from the Drawer of Knowledge?"

"The Drawer of Knowledge?" they'd ask skeptically.

"Yes," I'd say. And I'd walk over to our cutting table and open a drawer, and I'd pull out a square I'd created and say, "Watch this. All we're doing is sewing straight from here to here. If you do this, and you sew all the way around here and cut this diagonally, you're going to get these four blocks."

I was showing them how to do a half square triangle or a Dresden plate, and I would show them just how easy it was, which gave them confidence to try it themselves. They would have a good time and leave the shop with a good feeling.

**THE DRESDEN IS** a quilt block that looks like a big dinner plate with points all the way around. And it's made in wedges. It used to be that these were all curved, and you would sit and turn under all the edges. Well, I discovered that if you take anything that's flat, fold it in half, and sew across the top, it'll peak. So we made a template. And that makes it so much easier to put together.

I have always loved sharing knowledge, and I love creating the kind of excitement that builds confidence in people when they learn a new idea or a new skill. I also knew that people wanted a reason to get together, so I came up with an idea to teach some quilting myself, and to make it fun. I called it the Friday Night Sew, and I offered it to anyone who wanted to come—at no charge. The importance of giving away the knowledge I had seemed obvious to me. If nothing else, I thought it might generate some more interest in our new business. After all, whoever came to a Friday Night Sew to make quilts might hire me to do their machine quilting.

No sooner did I ask a few friends and family members to help spread the word about Friday nights than a few people actually showed up—and suddenly we had a little community of quilters, quilting together, at the Missouri Star Quilting Company. I loved seeing the smiles on their faces when they learned a new shortcut. I loved seeing the pride these women had—and the occasional man too—when they finished a quilt they'd been working on for a long time. It turned out to be so much more than a little promotion for the shop. I loved teaching. It felt good. And it was *fun*.

# Casting Bread
# upon the Water

In November, Alan lost his job with a major software corporation. He was a little nervous about what he was going to do next but also really excited about the idea of putting more time and energy into building my little quilting shop into something bigger—and maybe something much more profitable than any of us ever could have imagined.

He started doing some research, and what he discovered is that the quilting world—unlike a lot of other popular crafts and businesses—hadn't yet made the leap to the online world. He was staying with a friend named Dave Mifsud up in Canada at the time. He and Dave had met during their mission work in Ukraine, and Dave was steeped in the worlds of business and marketing. So Alan recruited him to help out.

After spending time looking at what was happening (and not happening) with quilting online, Alan decided we should have a website to get people interested and let more people know that the shop existed. He built that website himself.

Then one day, he said, "Mom, I want you to film some tutorials."

"Oh, that's great, honey," I said. "What's a tutorial?"

He explained to me that a tutorial was a video of me showing people how to quilt. There were people gaining all sorts of "followers" on YouTube, and making a lot of money, just by teaching people how to do things they would have had to go to school for in the past, from fixing cars to playing guitar.

"You want to put me on YouTube?" I asked. "Isn't that for young people?"

"No, Mom," he said. "It's for everybody." He explained that there really wasn't anyone on YouTube teaching quilting. All he had found were a few rough videos that were all done in close-up, just showing some anonymous person's hands holding a needle and thread or cutting fabric in a certain shape. But Alan got this idea in his head (for some reason!) that I might be able to offer tutorials that were a bit more fun and interesting.

We were about six months into the business and had finished painting the walls and dressing the shop up for making these videos when Alan showed up with a video camera.

"Mom, let's give a tour. We're going to show Dave what we've got down here. Where the money is going," he said.

Dave had been actively helping us try to build the business, but he had never been down from Canada to see us in person.

"Sure, Al. Okay," I said.

The first time we recorded, I was pretty stiff. I just didn't know what he wanted me to do. Al said we had to shoot it again, and gave me some instruction, and the second time I was more relaxed.

"All right, Mom, that was awesome! Way to go, there it is!" Al said.

Then he realized that he hadn't turned on the video camera. It was off the whole time.

"Mom," he said apologetically, "we're going to try this one more time."

When we tried it again, I was coming into my theater element, so I was prancing around and being a little over-the-top when I spun around, and my leg got caught in a big cord. Next thing I knew, I was on the ground.

I didn't get up.

"Mom? Are you okay?"

"No. I'm not," I said. I was laughing, but I said, "I really think I hurt myself."

"Yeah, whatever, Mom," Al said. I was such a kidder, and he was so used to me joking around, that he didn't believe me!

"No. Al, I really think I broke my leg," I said.

"What do you want me to do? Call 911?"

"Yes. Al. Could you *please* call 911?"

"Mom, we can't have an ambulance come to the quilt shop!" he said.

"Okay. Well, I think I need to go to the doctor."

He tried to get me up, but I couldn't walk on my leg at all. Somehow he was able to lift me up and get me into the van, and we drove over to the clinic.

"Yes, it's broken," they said.

They put me in a boot right there in the office—and told me I needed to stay off it.

The shop was barely up and running. We couldn't afford to close the doors and miss even one quilting job, or we might not have been able to pay Sarah's second-mortgage payment. So, the next day, with no quilting experience at all, Natalie got thrown into the business full-time. She had been there to help and support me from the beginning, but now we needed her there daily. As I mentioned earlier, Natalie had five children by this time, so half of the time we weren't sure she would make it in; and it was nearly impossible to hold her accountable for being late to a temporary job, when we were paying her zero dollars to get up and go there every day. But she did it. She stepped in to help. And every day she would call me up from the shop and ask, "How do I do this?" or "What do I do now?"

I was so used to getting up and doing whatever I needed to do, it was hard for me to stay home and stay still. I learned quickly that I don't do crutches very well. They hurt my armpits. They hurt my hands. So I preferred to just crawl everywhere.

There I was, in a boot, home from the doctor's office, after crawling up from the driveway, up the front porch, up the stairs, and finally into bed. Ron had helped get me up there and then he put pillows up under my leg. I was resting after I had taken some pain medication, so I was feeling pretty good after a few days when all of a sudden, here comes Al.

"Mom," he said, "I'm only home for a few more days, and we have to film."

"Al, no. I broke my leg!" I said.

"Mom, *please*. You could do it sitting down."

And because a mother always wants to please her kids, I sighed, pulled on some clothes, crawled out of bed, and crawled back down the stairs. I was on the floor when they brought me my grandmother's wheelchair, but no one stopped to think about the fact that my grandmother was probably four feet eleven. She was this tiny woman, and here I was at five feet ten! The seat on that chair was so small. But we did it. I made it to the shop, and we filmed the first few tutorials with me in a boot, with a broken leg, squished in a tiny little wheelchair with crutches in the background, struggling to enunciate because of the effects of the pain medication.

But we made the tutorial videos fun—and people noticed.

WHEN WE STARTED WITH THE tutorials on YouTube, we were just a quilting shop providing a service. All we hoped we'd get out of it was new customers—that if somebody made a quilt from the lessons I'd taught them, then hopefully they would send their quilt to me for the long-arm finishing. That truly was our only goal. And that was unusual.

In the quilting world, designers generally didn't want people to use or copy their patterns unless they paid for them. It makes sense. Those patterns are someone's original creative works of art—not unlike songs, or poems.

I didn't feel the same way about what I was creating. I wanted people to go share my patterns, and to use whatever I taught them in my tutorials to create quilts in whatever fabrics or colors they chose, and to hopefully encourage other people to use those patterns too. I couldn't control the price of the fabric they would use. We didn't sell any fabrics. But I *could* control what I did with the education.

And I chose to *give it away*.

A whole lot of people, including fabric-store and quilting-shop owners who found my tutorials on YouTube, were uncomfortable with that at first. They looked up our website and called the shop, or sent me emails asking nervously, "Is it okay if I use this?"

"Yes!" I'd say. "We want you to use this! You can teach it in your shops, in your guilds, in your stores. You can make it in your fabric, and kit it up in your fabric, share it, send it out to your customers. You can have this class forever. We would just like you to say, 'We got this from the Missouri Star Quilt Company,' in the hopes that people might send us their quilts when they're ready to be machine-quilted."

Within weeks, we had people tell us they were able to sell out their fabrics by doing just that. They were shocked, and they were so grateful—and so were we.

"Why would you let us do this?" they asked.

"Because there's enough for everybody!" I'd tell them. "My mother would always say, 'When you cast your bread upon the water, it comes back buttered.'"

I truly believe that saying applies to business as much as it does in life.

So I started filming on a regular basis, with Jake stepping in to do the camera work when Alan wasn't around. And one day a lady called up and said, "That fabric you showed in that last tutorial? I'd like some of that."

"Well, it's my fabric. You can't have it," I said.

"No, I want to buy it," she clarified.

"Well, hmmm. I don't even remember where I got that fabric."

"You don't sell it?"

"No. We're not selling fabric. We're just teaching you things, and then I can machine-quilt your quilt for you on the long-arm machine."

That's when I had a lightbulb moment, as Alan had when this whole idea started. I immediately called up Sarah and Al and said, "You know what? We should probably sell some fabric."

They both agreed, and that sent us on our next learning adventure.

OUR LITTLE SHOP COULDN'T SEEM to get much traction with the big fabric companies through our online research and phone calls. But one day we discovered that there was a market in Houston, Texas, where shops like ours could buy fabric at wholesale prices, directly from the wholesalers. So Natalie, Sarah, and I decided to make the fourteen-hour drive to Houston in an old Suburban.

When we got to the market, we were waiting in a long line when the lady in front of us said, "We're going to open a quilt shop and we only have about $80,000 to invest."

We overheard that and looked at each other with our eyebrows raised to the roof, and I thought, *We don't have that kind of money.* We had no idea that it might cost that much to get started selling fabric—and we also knew that we didn't want to go any further in debt.

In Houston, we quickly learned that to buy a line of fabric, which is about twenty different fabrics, you have to buy a bolt of every one, even at the market. Some companies would allow you to buy fabric yardage, but even that was five dollars a yard wholesale, and there were fifteen yards on a bolt, and twenty bolts that you would have to buy. We didn't have that kind of money on us. We didn't even have *hundreds* of dollars on us. We weren't millionaires. We weren't even *thousandaires*, you know?

So we left the market and went to the Moda Fabrics warehouse instead, where Sarah spent every last penny of her personal savings on discount fabric—just so we'd have *something* to sell at the shop.

We still enjoyed our adventure to the market, and we dropped our Missouri Star Quilt Company business cards at every designer's booth. We hoped we might hear from some of them once we got back home. But nobody called, and nobody came to see us, until several months later when one day I was alone in our little shop, and a gentleman poked his head in the door.

He looked around with a curious look on his face and asked, "Is this a fabric shop?"

"It could be," I said. "We're a quilting company."

"Oh, good," he said. "Are you Sarah?"

"No, that's my daughter. She isn't here today."

"She called and asked me to come in," he said. "Are you the owner?"

"Yes. I'm Jenny. It's a family business."

"Ah. So, can I show you my fabric?"

"Yes!" I said. "I'd love to see."

He was carrying a large brown suitcase, like the Avon Lady or the Fuller Brush Man might've carried in the olden days. But this suitcase was full of fabric samples. He started to pull out these samples and laid all the different pieces down together, and they were so beautiful. I fell in love with them. He started telling me about the quality and craftsmanship, and I started feeling guilty for taking up this man's time.

"I'm sorry," I said. "We just can't afford fabric. And I feel so guilty because you keep pulling this out, and I want it. I want it all, but I can't afford it."

"What do you mean you can't afford it?" he asked.

I said, "We don't want to do the debt thing, you know?"

"Oh," he said.

I could see that he was still thinking about how he could sell me something after having come all the way to Hamilton from wherever he'd come from. And as he started to pack all those beautiful fabrics back into his big brown suitcase, he stopped.

"Well," he said, "have you thought about these precuts?"

# 17

# Tiny Squares
# & Good Friends

As soon as those words came out of his mouth, a light went off in my brain: I had used some precut fabrics for a table runner before. Precuts were one small square from every fabric in a line. They were cut to size, and the colors went together, so they could be sewn into quilts real easy. And then you could buy one bolt of fabric for a border around it and you could finish your project without having to buy a whole lot of fabric, and without going through all the work of cutting out every single piece of it yourself. I loved it! It was so easy. And best of all, it was much less expensive.

*We could do this!* I thought. We could *sell* these. And if we needed smaller pieces, I could cut them out of one of the squares, and then maybe we could bring in some white fabric, or a background piece to go with the squares. We could give my tutorial customers what they want without having to buy twenty bolts of fabric at a time.

I asked him to please give me four of his packets of precuts.

"You can't buy *four*," he said. "You have to buy these charm packs, in packs of twenty-four."

"Okay then, I'll try to find a shop to split it with me because we'll *never* sell more than four," I said. At that point we were relying on people coming into our little shop, and we hadn't even tried to sell anything online besides our service. I honestly would've been excited to sell four precut bundles in all!

**IT TURNED OUT** that Sarah was about ten steps ahead of me. She had remembered me using precuts, and she had asked this salesman to come in and show us the line. I was clueless, but it sure worked out well!

From what I heard, the idea of selling packages of precuts started when one of the designers at a company called Kansas Troubles created a line of fabric that looked like the classic country fabric used in what are called Nickel Quilts. And the Nickel Quilt pattern uses five-inch squares. The designer had this idea to give everybody one five-inch square from every fabric in her line.

The salesman who came to see us at our little shop in Hamilton had not sold very many of them. I was one of the first people to show interest in this new idea—along with Sarah—mostly because it was something we thought we could afford to buy.

Over time, people who were fans of Nickel Quilts discovered these precuts from Kansas Troubles and went nuts for them. They sold so many that they started making them in other sizes too. And selling precuts turned into a big part of MSQC's growth.

I told Alan about these precuts and suggested that I could talk about them in my tutorials online; then we could sell the bundled precuts so whoever watched the tutorial could then make that quilt.

"Well, couldn't we cut fabric and bundle it ourselves, so we could sell these precut packages for whatever quilt you're making, to go with whatever tutorial you give?" he asked.

It just made so much sense: we could sell kits of precuts to viewers, so they could basically order a box from us that would have all the fabrics they needed to make the quilt I just showed them how to make!

With Dave on board, who invested his sweat equity into marketing and finance for us, plus Alan's ability to create our website from scratch and get the precuts listed, we were off and running in no time.

Actually, we were more like off and standing. When the website went up, nothing happened. No one came. We didn't sell a thing.

For days and days, Sarah and Natalie and I kept hitting *refresh* on the computer, hoping to see a sale. David and Alan did the same thing from their workspace up in Canada, and over and over there was nothing.

Then, one day, three weeks after the website launched, there was *one*. A single sale!

It was my niece who logged on and made that first purchase, but still, we were *so excited*. Alan called up within seconds to tell me we'd made our first sale, and I said, "I know! We were online too!" We all celebrated.

That same week, a few other friends and neighbors made purchases, too, which was just so wonderful. It always feels good to be supported. But we were still racking our brains trying to figure out how to get more of the folks who were watching my tutorials to come on over and buy something from our website.

First, we tried to make the tutorials as appealing as possible to as wide of an audience as possible. We wanted to speak to beginners who'd never picked up a needle and thread, and also speak to experienced quilters who needed some additional inspiration or could learn to speed up the process using some of the shortcuts from my Drawer of Knowledge.

Thankfully, I'd had plenty of practice in this sort of thing. In all my years of homeschooling, I had to find a way to make lessons appeal to our youngest, our oldest, and everyone in between. Now I was just doing it online, to an audience that kept growing every week.

"Hi! I'm Jenny from Missouri Star Quilt Company, and today I'm going to show you how to make a four patch," I'd say. Alan would turn off the camera. "Mom, stop. I don't know what a four patch is."

I realized we had our own language, and I had to simplify it. So we'd start again. "Today I'm going to take four squares that are the same size. Two are gonna be a light color, two are gonna be a dark color. I'm going to sew light to dark and dark to light and it's going to make a block we call the four patch."

We didn't script anything, we didn't overthink it. I just got up and did what I knew how to do. I suppose I'm an entertainer by nature. I saw this as entertaining as much as it was teaching, and the feedback we received backed that up. The audience loved that I was real. They loved it when I made mistakes on camera and then tried to make the best of it. Quilting was fun for me, and I wanted to make sure it looked fun to anyone who might have been scrolling around the web and happened to find us.

When it came to making sure the tutorials looked really good, that's where Jake jumped in. Alan's idea of an overhead shot was to stand up real tall and hold the camera pointing down at my quilting table. But Jake came in and built a rig so we could hang the camera and get a perfect overhead shot. He set up lights so everything would look bright and cheery, and there wouldn't be shadows everywhere. And he started brainstorming ideas for contests to get viewers more engaged. Actually, all the kids started throwing out new ideas, and we tried 'em all, including setting a flat-rate shipping price of five dollars for anything we sold.

Then one day, out of the blue yet again, we made eight sales in a row. We sold out of every charm pack (the precut packages) of the Crazy Eights fabric line we carried.

Alan and David and Sarah all started clicking to see where the sales came from and what might have spurred the sudden run on our little store—and they quickly realized that those items had been mispriced. Somehow we had listed them for $.88 apiece instead of $2.88.

The way I looked at it, we either just lost a bunch of money, or we'd have to tell those customers that the price was a mistake and they needed to pay the full price if they still wanted to buy them. Either way, I was sure that mistake was going to hurt us.

"Not really," Alan assured me. "Most of these customers bought more than just the Daily Deal, and with the shipping fee we still made a little money on each sale—even *after* that really deep discount."

"Plus," he said, "now they're customers. Hopefully they'll tell their friends what a great deal they got, and they'll come back and buy more."

Alan was right. That's exactly what happened.

Sarah wrapped all eight of those items like presents before we shipped them out and included a handwritten note in every one of them: "Thank you so much for shopping with us. We really appreciate your business!" (We still do that to this day. No matter who packs up a box for shipping, they include a handwritten note thanking our customers for shopping with us.)

And from that day forward, we put up a Daily Deal on our MSQC website offering something for a very deep discount—all the way up to 100 percent off sometimes (plus shipping). And customers loved it. They still do. They kept coming back, and word spread all over the quilting world, and all sorts of customers came to the site to buy us out of every deal we offered. They bought up other items while they were shopping too. The kids figured out how we could start offering some quilting supplies on our website—thread, cutting tools, and other items we could sell without spending a fortune up front to buy them from the wholesalers—and we sold those, and we took in more and more quilts on the long-arm each week, and all of a sudden things started to get really busy.

Once we started offering fabric, we grew at such a rapid rate we could barely keep up. We would stay up all night cutting, and I can cut fabric fast, but it wasn't fast enough. Everyone in the family had to chip in just to get the orders out the door. We even got the little children involved. I set up tables as if we were a little factory in the back part of the shop, and to anybody who was between six and twenty I'd say, "Fold, iron, tag, fold!" We had them all working, and they thought it was so much fun. They loved doing it. But everything we did, we *had* to do. Very few of the fabric companies were willing to do precuts for us then, even though the demand for precuts was clearly there and we proved that with the number of orders that came in from our customers every time we posted a new tutorial. It was all up to us.

None of us got paid for doing this work. Every penny we made we poured right back into the business. We just hoped that, soon enough, the business would start sustaining itself in a way that we might be able to hire some employees.

In the meantime, we got help from some unexpected sources right there in our local community.

Bernice and Delores were some of our very first customers. They were two retired sisters who didn't even own a sewing machine. They sewed quilts by hand, and once every two weeks they would bring us a huge, queen-sized, handmade quilt for me to quilt on the long arm.

At first I asked, "Why do you want me to machine-quilt this when you sewed it by hand? Don't you want to hand-quilt it?"

"Oh, no. We don't do that," they answered. "We just sew these pieces together."

Bernice is the younger sister, and the shorter sister, with short, curly gray hair. Delores is a few years older with straight, long gray hair that she always wears back in a ponytail or braids. And it's no exaggeration to say they kept the lights on for us in our first year. They were two of our most loyal customers, out of so many customers who we'll never forget—who trusted us with their quilts.

But they gave us much more than some steady work. They discovered the shop when we first opened up, and they fell in love with our family. They were among the first ones who came to Friday Night Sew, and they always brought a special snack or some good, yummy thing that they made for us to eat. They're both such nurturing women, and we needed that so much for our little company. They loved every one of my children, and they loved me, and it was just the sweetest thing the way they wanted to help us. They very clearly wanted to see us succeed, as did several other friends and locals that came in and helped us as well.

We had church friends show up, and quilt-group friends, and neighbors. Local business owners offered to help out. New customers became friends, and volunteered to help when we needed it, too, and the closest we could come to paying any of them was to give them some fabric in return for their time. It all meant so much to me. To the whole family.

Not everyone believed we could grow a successful business in Hamilton, though. We had comments from some folks, including a delivery man or two, who thought we were crazy. The thought (which they sometimes shared right out loud) was, "No one comes to Hamilton to shop. How can you possibly do enough business here to stay in business?"

Some folks also thought we would have a tough time because we started right after the economy crashed. But as luck would have it, our timing could not have been better. When things like a stock market crash happen, or any sort of event that shakes up life as we know it, people tend to go back to basics. Sewing is a basic. Quilting is a basic. At Christmastime, and for birthdays, people don't have the money to go out and buy a hundred presents anymore. But they can feel good about giving the gift of something made with their hands. It feels good to work with your hands, to be able to start something from scratch and see it completed. There's something soothing about it. Comforting.

And it didn't take long for customers to respond. We were maybe six months after the website launch when our dear friend Carolyn Peterson, who worked in the antique shop in the center of town, arranged for a busload of folks to come visit us from Iowa. It was a small bus. It only held maybe forty people, but Carolyn managed to spread the word through a fabric shop in the region, and she sold just about every seat. The idea was to give folks a day's worth of fun sewing activities, so the whole family chipped in and made the shop look real pretty, and my friend Joleen made food so we could serve lunch, and we cleared out the back room so we could set up chairs we borrowed from church. It turned into my very first Trunk Show, where I stood up in front of the group and showed them how to make a few projects. Two of the projects weren't even quilts! It was a tea-towel apron and a pillowcase. But I also showed them a new method I developed for making half-square triangles, and how to make Dresden plates the easy way. We put together kits of every fabric they would need to make those projects if they wanted to—and we sold every kit we made. It was a huge success!

I never, ever would have predicted that just a few years later, we'd have four, five, six large buses full of quilters coming to Hamilton from all around the country, every day of the week during the summer months. But based on that first bus trip, we all agreed that we were off to a pretty good start.

Still, there was one moment when the true meaning of what we were doing, and of who we were reaching, became absolutely clear to me.

It wasn't very long after Alan had uploaded a handful of my tutorials online, and they were just beginning to get noticed on YouTube, when a girl from Brazil called the shop. This woman said, "I have to meet you."

"You're calling from Brazil?" I said.

"Yes!" she said. "You taught me to quilt. You taught me this skill. It changed my life!"

And now, she said, she wanted to come finish her quilt with me, on my machine.

"You want to come to the United States?" I said. "For a quilt?"

I couldn't wrap my head around it.

A few weeks later, she flew all the way from Brazil, and when she walked into our little shop—in the middle of nowhere, across the street from a vacant auto shop with a broken-down car in the yard, and a few blocks away from a Dollar General— she was beside herself. We spent the whole afternoon together quilting this beautiful quilt she had carried with her across the globe. She shared her personal story with me, and we shared this incredible sense of joy and love and pride as we finished the last stitch of her quilt together in my little shop.

For someone to come all those miles to meet me, all because of what I had taught her to do, in a tutorial, online—that changed everything.

If MSQC hadn't grown into what it is today, if we never expanded beyond that one little long-arm shop, if that one woman from Brazil had been the only woman whose life I'd touched through my work, it would've been enough for me.

It would have been enough.

# 18

# Family First

The Hamilton post office is only a couple of blocks away from our original shop, and when things first started to sell online, we used to walk down with a couple of packages to send. As business picked up, we'd find ourselves walking down with a bag full of packages. Then we had to drive down, because the post office gave us these big heavy mailing bags to put them in, and then all of a sudden one day we had a *hundred* packages. Morgan, who was one of our first hires, and who did our shipping and our cleaning, laid in the middle of them and we took a picture of her, like, "We sold a hundred things today!" And then we got so busy that the post office started picking up from *us*. That was such a big thing for us. They'd come once a day. Then they'd come twice a day.

We were still in that one building. We turned the room in the back into a warehouse of sorts, and shipping happened in the middle room, around the long-arm machine at first. We had to figure out how to get boxes, how to get tape. Do we write all the names? Do we print all the names? Alan got us a printer. We had to get a little scale to weigh things on, because every package was different. And it was Alan and Sarah and Jake who had to figure out all those things, and how to afford all of those things without losing money on the sales.

I truly left the business side of things up to them. I'm just not good at it. If it were up to me, I'd give away the farm every day. But thanks to their hard work, we were able to set up an account with a wholesaler and start to offer all sorts of fabric on our website. There was one problem with that: we were completely out of room. So Sarah, Alan, and David decided we'd better expand, and we were lucky enough to know someone who owned a perfect spot, who was ready to sell. They purchased the old antiques shop from our friend Teresa Ford; the shop where Carolyn Peterson worked! It had big front windows, and it was right around the corner and across the street on Hamilton's main street, where we could set up a proper quilting store—the kind of place where customers could come in and have room to browse a selection of fabrics, and where we could store a whole lot of fabric at once. The old shop would be used entirely for our shipping operation.

So now we had a whole new space to figure out, and we didn't know the first thing about how to put a retail store together. But none of us ever thought for a second that we couldn't do it. We believed in each other. We each brought skills to the table, and we relied on and trusted each other.

Ron was still working his job. Sarah's husband, Seth, was still working his job. But they worked nights and weekends to help remodel that shop. Having spouses all around us who supported us and believed in us allowed us to keep growing the business in the first few years. That made such a difference.

We bought a whole bunch of big old shelves from the local library, which we thought would be perfect for displaying bolts of fabric in the new shop—and we realized, after we'd moved them, that they weren't deep enough to hold bolts of fabric. They didn't work for us at all. Then Alan had an idea for a shelf on casters, thinking his design would allow us to rearrange the store easily and change things up now and then. It was made so you could display fabric on both sides. But we needed to build a bunch of these shelves, and Ron and Seth just didn't have time to get it done after work and on weekends.

That's when Bernice and Delores came to the rescue.

"Our husbands are handy," they said. "They can help you build these shelves."

So James and Bob, both retired as well, came over. They looked at our space and listened to what we needed, then they made a jig so that we could cut out a whole bunch of shelves and make sure they were all identical. It had never even occurred to us to do that. They came in and worked every day. They brought their own tools. We had all this plywood, so they cut out piece after piece of wood to build shelves for the fabric. Then they screwed the casters on, screwed the sides on, screwed the shelves on. They made eighty sets of shelves between them!

James said to me one day, "I go home at night and my hands hurt so bad. I haven't done this stuff for twenty years. Dolores pours vinegar on them and the vinegar helps relax my hands. And then I come back and do this all again. And you ain't even paying me!"

"You don't have to do it, James," I said. "Really. You don't have to do it. We'll do it."

"No, no," he said. "We've got to help you *kids*. We can't let you do this on your own."

They were so sweet to us.

As all of this was going on, I was still doing all this quilting on the long-arm machine. And when a quilt gets finished being quilted, sometimes customers wanted to pay us to do the binding. (That's the fabric that wraps all the way around the outer edges of the quilt, sealing up the edges of the top, the batting, and the backing after it's quilted.) So I was doing that too. And one day Bernice and Delores came in and said, "You look so tired. Can we help you bind? Can we do that?"

Those two women and so many people in our little community were such a gift. I offered them fabric and anything else I could in return for their time, and they just graciously thanked me and the kids for allowing them to help. Their husbands did the same. It was wonderful.

One day after the new shop opened, I found myself running out of time to put a new front window display together, so I asked Bernice and Delores if they wouldn't mind doing the binding at a little table in the front window. They were thrilled! They sat there as people walked by, waving at them, stopping with children to watch as they worked. It might have been one of the most fun window displays we ever had.

They kept coming in a couple of days a week, and kept binding and binding. Eventually they would get paid for the beautiful work they did, but they did it mostly because they loved having something meaningful to do. And we were so glad to have them because they brought so much joy to the customers, and our family, and our employees. They're like everybody's grandma or everybody's mom. How wonderful would life be if every shop and every company had a Bernice and Delores of their own!

A lan started this business for me. He had no intention of making it his full-time job, and he didn't. As MSQC was growing, he tried to build a niche for himself in the consulting world. He was traveling to Pittsburgh and St. Louis, working for start-ups and corporations that he thought would make our little hometown business look like small potatoes.

So when Sarah, or Natalie, or I called him with a problem that needed solving, he understandably got a little frustrated. But we had to call him.

Growing a business isn't all fun, and growing a family-run business presents special challenges. For Alan, trying to grow MSQC mostly from afar while he continued to work as a consultant meant sometimes he'd return to town like a storm. Sarah, Natalie, Jake, and I were all working in our own ways, but Al was the boss. And when he showed up, he would whirl in and have all these new ideas about things. We grew so fast and Alan was making so many changes that it felt like everything was in constant upheaval.

For a long time Alan was the bad guy in the company, which was really hard for him as he is such a joyful person by nature. But a growing company with employees needs discipline, and the fact that we were a family led to some tense moments. Like the time I'd been working all day and I was thirsty, so I took some change out of the drawer to get a soda. Alan came right up to me and said, "Mom, if you take money out of the register and you spend it on yourself, it's embezzling!"

I looked up at him with tired eyes, then took a breath and said, "Alan, you're not my boss, you're my son!" Here I was working day and night, long hours, and giving it all my heart, energy, and time, and my son who I took care of all his life was reprimanding me for a soda!

"Well, I'm your boss too," he said flatly. "And this has to work."

**ONE DAY, WHILE** Alan was consulting for a start-up group, the wife of one of the group's investors asked him, "What do you do?" He told her a little bit about his consulting work, and he mentioned that he also started a family quilting business. Well, when she heard the word "quilting" she stopped him and said, "Oh my gosh, I follow this woman online and I love her! She taught me how to quilt! Her name is Jenny. Jenny Doan. Do you know her?"

"Well, yes," said Alan with a surprised smile. "That's my mom."

Later that same night, he snuck away for a moment to text me: "Mom, you are officially more famous than I am."

We didn't hire an HR person until we had 115 employees. Sarah and Alan did all the hiring and firing themselves through all of our company's rapid growth. Because Alan put so much on the line for this company, he'll admit there were times when he became hyper-critical of anyone he thought wasn't giving it their all on the job.

Sometimes he would come in and have to fire those people. We all felt bad and would try to change his mind: "Alan, no, he's a good guy. He's got a family. He's got kids. You can't fire him!" And he'd say, "Well, he was actually sleeping on the job for an hour today. He's fired."

We might not have liked it, but it was Alan's dedication and his demeanor that grew the business to what it would eventually become. And it was Alan who was the big risk-taker, and who managed so much of our growth. As I've said, if it was left up to me I would've stayed a long-armer and we'd still be in our first little shop quilting for the local people.

When business decisions led to disagreements between the kids, I had to keep reminding them that family matters most. So when things got rough, as they do, I reminded them of the blanket fight the girls had back in Greenfield, or the mock trial we held with Ron as the judge when they were teenagers.

"Yes, Mom," they said with a sigh. "We remember."

Even when they argued, they were able to work things out, and heal and move on, not only for the sake of the business, but for the sake of our family.

Of course, as a rule, I'm someone who believes it's worth trying to be kind and to work things out with everybody we meet in life too.

Not long after we opened the shop, there was a customer who came in who got angry.

"I came all the way out of my way to visit this shop, and you have almost nothing here!" she complained. It was true. We didn't have much to sell in the beginning. But just before she stormed out the door, she kicked a bolt of fabric with her foot and shouted, "This is so ugly!"

I had a friend who was helping us at the time and she came up to me and said, "You do not pay me enough to wait on someone like her."

"Oh dear," I said. "Well, if she comes in again, let's try something different. We are going to be so nice to her, she's not even going to know what to do about it."

Lo and behold, the lady came back, and the next time she came in we could tell right away that she was in a sour mood again. My friend came back to my desk and told me she was there, so I went right up to her.

"Hi," I said. "How are you?"

At first she was short and huffy, but I persisted.

"What do you do for work?" I asked. "Tell me about *you*. Tell me about yourself."

It didn't take long for her to start pouring out her story, and that's when I learned that she lived alone, she had never married, and she was very unhappy working a job where she felt unappreciated. She was coming through our little town regularly because her parents had left her some farmland that was a big responsibility. The bottom line is she felt she never had any time to do anything she wanted to do herself.

It occurred to me that her little detours to our store were, in part, her heart looking for the same thing we all look for: connection.

She didn't buy anything that day, but she kept coming back— mostly, I think, because we wrapped her up in kindness.

As our inventory grew, this woman started to notice a few fabrics that she didn't think were quite so "ugly," and she actually bought some. "I love to come in here," she said one day. And then we found out that she wasn't even quilting. She was buying our fabric, but she never made anything! So my friend took some of the fabrics we knew she liked and she made her a little wall quilt.

"I know you love this fabric," my friend said as she handed it to her, "so I thought you might like this."

Our onetime angry customer was moved to tears.

A few months later, she came in and sat down across from me as I was working at my desk. "This shop has changed my life," she said. "I want you to know that. It's really changed my life."

"Yeah?" I said. "How?"

"Well, you were so nice to me. Even when *I* wasn't nice."

She fell silent for a moment, and then she said, "I have to tell you something."

I could tell by her voice that it was important, so I stopped what I was doing and listened.

"I have some news," she said, "and I don't really want to go through this by myself."

"What is it?" I asked.

"I have breast cancer."

I stood up, walked around the desk, and wrapped my arms around her. I don't think anybody had hugged her in a very long time. And as I held her, I thought about the first time she came in. I thought about how we could have gone to the back room and said, "She's horrible," and we could have told her, "Don't ever come in here again." Instead, I decided that we should try kindness. I decided to see "What happens if?"

And look what happened.

That's actually one of my favorite creative questions in quilting: "What happens if?" What happens if we try something different? What happens if we turn this around? What happens if we go in another direction, or cut across this fold?

But I've found that using that creative question in life has mattered just as much, and sometimes more, when it comes to people. And I treasure the people that we've been so blessed to get to know through this business.

As Missouri Star Quilting Company continued to grow, I did my best to pass that positive attitude on to every employee we hired, and especially to those who worked on our sales floors or in our customer service department. I encouraged every employee to be good to everybody. Sometimes customers get angry. Sometimes employees get angry too! We all make mistakes. Mistakes happen. When they do, we own up to them. We try to make it right. And we do it with grace and kindness.

That's quite a shock to some people. Grace and kindness are not what people have come to expect in today's world. And guess what? It isn't just good for me and my family. It's good for business too.

19

# Eighteen-Wheelers & Hurricane Love

Every week, every time I put up a new tutorial, our online business grew. And it was getting harder and harder to keep track of all the inventory, and to get it shipped out.

I finally called Alan one day and said, "Alan, we cannot sell this if we can't ship it fast enough. We have to get that part figured out because I don't want people waiting two weeks for us to find something. We also can't sell things if we're running out of things all the time," I said.

Al had been developing a network of business professionals, and right around this time he happened to be meeting with another entrepreneur who had become one of his mentors. He expressed his frustration with the amount of time he was spending dealing with this little "side business" he had started for his mother, and when Al told him the details about what was going on, his mentor looked at him and said, "Do you have any idea how many entrepreneurs would give their *eyeteeth* for something that has that kind of momentum?"

The outcome of that conversation was huge: Alan decided to give MSQC his full-time effort, and so did Dave. (Sarah had been fully committed from day one.)

A whole bunch of Dave's family members decided to get involved, too, beginning with his sister April (in product); his dad, Dave Sr. (in product and inventory management, and one of our biggest cheerleaders); and continuing with his wife, Elisabeth (who handled Pinterest in the beginning); his brother Mike (who started as our CFO and is now our CEO); and Mike's wife, Katie (who writes the Daily Deal); also Camille (a writer), who is Katie's sister, and Colin (an analyst), who is April's husband. Their family blended seamlessly with ours, and they brought their own unique set of skills to the company.

Alan came back to Hamilton and hired a contractor, and he got to work building us a shipping warehouse across the bridge on the other side of town; the kind of place that would be filled with employees, and have to meet certain state and federal standards, and be up to code in every way.

In the middle of it all, Al came in and sat down at my desk, and he's this big, tall, bearded, successful businessman at this point, but he put his head in his hands like a troubled kid and said, "What am I doing? I don't know anything about building a warehouse. How can I build a warehouse? Even the drinking fountains have to be in a certain place, at a certain height. Things have to be just so."

I looked at him and I said, "Alan, God told Noah how to build a boat. Now you go into that office and pray, and don't come out until you know how to build a warehouse."

He laughed a little and said, "You might be onto something, Mom."

I think sometimes, no matter how confusing things seem, or how busy they get, taking a little time to stop and think, and pray (if that's what you do), makes all the difference in the world.

Alan ended up building us a warehouse. He hired an inventory and shipping manager too. And no sooner was that warehouse up and running than Alan did the projections, based on the growth we'd seen, and he realized we needed a *bigger* warehouse—a warehouse capable of potentially handling thousands of packages per day. So he hired a COO with warehouse and shipping experience, and we built a new warehouse that would carry us through all the growth that was still to come. Growth we couldn't have even imagined when we first got started. Our warehouse now ships out around ten thousand packages per day! We have big-rig eighteen-wheeler trucks backed up to the bays, and we fill them from front to back, top to bottom, with nothing but Missouri Star packages heading off to find new homes with our customers.

It all happens here in Hamilton, Missouri, and every one of those packages still has a handwritten note inside from the employee who packed up the box. Because every one of us is still thankful for every order we receive, and every customer we have.

As our business continued to expand, we purchased more vacant storefronts downtown and opened themed quilt shops in them all. Every type of fabric got its own shop!

Ron and Seth worked tirelessly to fix up all those buildings. They had to be completely gutted down to the studs; down to the footings on some of them. There were brick walls that had to be completely replaced. Floor joists and support beams that needed to be replaced too. They needed new wiring (thank goodness we had Seth!) and new plumbing, to bring them up to code. Most of the buildings were at risk of collapse before they put in that work, yet they brought every one of them back to life. (And once we could afford it, we hired a construction crew.)

As those shops opened up, one by one, we expanded our workforce, and we basically turned our little town into Quilt Town, USA. At the same time, we started to see the impact we were making far from our small-town community.

When a devastating hurricane swept across the Gulf of Mexico and slammed into eastern Texas, people in the quilt world wanted to help. Quilters are some of the most generous people you will ever meet. A lot of them don't have a ton, but they love to give what they can, and giving quilts away is a way to share love and comfort. But when this hurricane hit, a lot of quilters didn't know where to send their quilts. So on our website, I said, "Please send us your quilts for disaster relief."

Within a couple of weeks of putting up that notice, we received over eight thousand quilts! It took half our warehouse to house them.

Meg, our events coordinator at the time, started calling everybody she could think of in Houston to see who could accept these donated quilts. She called the Red Cross, the schools, the churches, and then we loaded all those quilts up in a big semi U-Haul truck, and she drove the truck to Houston herself.

"I cried at every stop," Meg told us.

She gave quilts to people whose homes had been destroyed, whose entire lives had been upended. She gave away all eight thousand quilts and the people who received them were so gracious, and so thankful. The stories she heard were heartbreaking, but the fact that all these people in the quilting community sent so many quilts to share their love to help comfort them meant the world.

And the quilts just kept on coming.

When she got home, I said, "I hate to tell you this, but there are four thousand more quilts in our warehouse."

"What am I going to do? I've called everyone I can think of," she said. "I don't know where else we can take them."

Well, because she was down there giving these beautiful quilts away, the word got around, and a day or two later a man called and said, "I hear you have some quilts to give away."

"I do," she said.

"I'm overseeing all the children refugees from Puerto Rico," where another devastating hurricane had blown through, "and they're so destitute, and they could sure use a quilt."

She asked, "How many do you need?"

"Well, that's the thing," he said. "I probably need about four thousand."

When the pastor at one of our little churches here heard that story, she was so moved, she rented a truck to deliver the four thousand quilts herself.

And ever since then, most of the churches in and around Hamilton have worked together in all sorts of ways to assist in our charitable efforts.

The reach of our company kept growing and growing, and I was so busy keeping up with everything in Hamilton and filming my weekly tutorials, I didn't even realize just how big it was getting.


ONE DAY IN 2015, ALAN told me, "Mom, we won the Best Small Business award for the state of Missouri!"

"Oh," I said. "Good job, honey. Good job."

He followed up to tell me, "We're up for the *national* Small Business award."

And I said, "That's great! Good job."

A few weeks later he said, "Mom, we're one of the contenders for the final four in the whole country!"

To me, a mom who had grown used to her kids getting accolades, I thought it was just another achievement. No big deal. We were all working hard and doing our best, and we didn't need outside awards to tell us that.

But then Alan told me we'd won! He and Sarah and our business partner Dave were invited to the White House to accept the award as National Small Business Persons of the Year.

For some reason that we can't even remember now, I wasn't invited to accompany them.

"Do you want to come to the White House?" Alan said. "I'm sure you can come. I'll call them."

"You know what, Al," I said, "it's really okay. It's no big deal to me because I'm going to teach in Wisconsin next week, at Nancy Zieman's! And that is a *huge* honor for me."

If you don't know, Nancy Zieman was one of the most amazing quilting people ever to live. She was the founder of Nancy's Notions, an author of more than forty sewing and quilting books, and host of the public television show *Sewing with Nancy*, the longest-running sewing program in North American television history.

It wasn't until I got to her event and Nancy stood up onstage to introduce me that I really understood what Alan was trying to tell me.

"Never in the history of our industry," Nancy said, "has any quilter been honored in the White House. Never in the history of our industry has anyone done what this family has done!"

She started listing off these big things that Missouri Star had accomplished, and I stood over to the side texting Al: "Al, I don't know if you know this, but this is *huge*!"

"Mom, I've been trying to tell you!" he texted back.

Since I couldn't go to the White House at that point, I made a quilt for them to give to the president.

"Please, please wear a suit," I begged Alan. He operated mostly in the Silicon Valley world, where it was acceptable to show up in a hoodie. But this was the White House!

He sent me a picture that morning. "Look, Mom. I'm wearing a suit!" he texted.

But later he texted: "Guess who didn't show up? The president."

Apparently President Obama was off touring a Nike factory that day.

*Dang it*, I thought. *The one time we got Alan to dress up.*

"Well, if he's not there to receive it, please bring that quilt home," I texted back.

President Obama could have had a real nice quilt for his bed.

They did take a nice picture of Alan, Sarah, and Dave with the quilt in front of the White House, though.

From there, it seemed like the awards and accolades just kept rolling in.

People would say to me all the time, "You did the most amazing job with these kids," and I was like, "I fed them." I mean, I'm sure what I did had *something* to do with it, but it wasn't like I said, "Today, we're going to make you a successful entrepreneur." It wasn't intentional in that way. I just loved them, and mothered them. They came with this skill set, and it was their job to make that skill set into everything it could be. I kept telling them, "If you can read, you can do anything," and I guess they took it to heart.

# Mr. Jenny &
# Trunk Show Tears

Ron kept working as a machinist at the *Kansas City Star* until MSQC had been up and running for about five years. That's when the company finally reached a point where it was not only sustaining itself and bringing in enough revenue to pay our employees, but was making enough of a profit for us to pay those of us in the family who had dedicated so much of our time to building the company from the start.

Ron retired, which was really hard for him at first, because all his life he had been out there slaying the dragons so that we could eat. And now he found himself at home, cooking, doing the laundry, running everybody's errands. He was picking up grandkids at school, fixing this or that when something broke, or building a shelf in one of our kids' homes. Whatever they needed, and whatever I needed, he was right on top of it, and he still is now. Which means he's not "retired" at all. He's working all the time!

Early on, it really did bother him that my salary was now paying for everything. But I said to him, "Honey, all your life you've done this and it was always 'our money.' You would've never said to me, 'You can't have this money.' This is exactly the same. It's 'our money.' It's not mine. It's not me bringing it home and *giving* it to you. This is our money because it was our money before. We created this family, and this business, *together*."

That seemed to make him feel a little better, but it's hard to break away from the old stereotypical roles. I've come to understand the reversing of those roles myself. I come home sometimes after a long day at work and I just want be like the guy in the '50s. I want to go, "Okay, I'm beat. I've had a hard day. Bring me my slippers and a pipe and I'm gonna read the paper 'til you fix my dinner."

The funny thing is, almost every day Ron will call me at work and say, "So, what do you want to have for dinner?"

It's just the two of us, and I'd be fine with a pre-cooked rotisserie chicken from the grocery store, and maybe a baked potato. I don't think fancy. I'm a good cook, but it's never been my favorite thing to do. Ron likes it! He'll start thinking about dinner plans early, and he likes the planning, and he likes making me something nice. He's the same way about handling most of the home stuff now. He's actually enjoyed the transition. He's happy that he gets the chance to support me as we keep growing this company, and that he gets to watch me have so much fun and get so much enjoyment while I do it.

Well, you know what that did for us? In every quilter's eyes, Ron became a hero. He is a champion, because he is the man they all wish they married. I know this because Ron travels with me everywhere I go, and sometimes the MSQC customers and fans are more excited to meet him than they are to meet me!

One of my absolute favorite things to do (before the pandemic hit in 2020) was Trunk Shows. Not everyone can come visit us in Hamilton. So with hundreds of thousands of subscribers to my YouTube channel and millions of views of my tutorials, I started getting asked to go out on the road to speak to quilting guilds, and then to larger and larger audiences at quilting conventions, and in towns and cities all over America.

I was happy to answer that call—and happy to have Ron by my side at every event.

By 2016, I was regularly selling out venues that held a thousand people. And what I'd do is show up, share some quilts, teach them how to make each one, and tell stories—not unlike the stories I've told here in this book. Only most of the stories were focused on quilting, and the healing power of quilting, and the community of quilters I meet everywhere I go who support each other and wrap so many people up in the love and caring they pour into this wonderful hobby of theirs. I would walk in with no script, and start talking, and sometimes I talked for more than two hours straight—and Ron was right there with me the whole time.

He became my sidekick. When we stood together onstage, he'd play the role of the spokesmodel who held up a quilt while I talked about it. He let me tease him and joke with him. And the audiences just loved it.

"The whole industry is jealous of my husband," I'd say, "because he will hold this quilt as long as I keep talking. And I'll keep talking a loooooooong time sometimes." I would start into a long-winded story, and they'd start laughing because Ron would act like his arms were getting weak, or he was falling asleep while standing up.

The quilters love him, and they love the way he supports me. So he has a following now. We went into a show one time and the whole front row full of women lifted up posters that said, "We love Mr. Jenny!"

They think he's all-that-and-a-bag-of-chips because he's such a good husband. And he is.

Every once in a while at one of those events somebody would say, "Tell us your story. Tell us the story of how you met." And that's such a humbling story. I'll tell you, going from town to town and city to city, one thing is certain: America fell in love with our family. Love is universal, and we all need more of it. People are hungry to see couples who love each other, and when they see us, and hear our story, it gives them hope.

I had a woman stand in line to meet me after one of these Trunk Shows, and of all the things she could have asked me about or told me, she said, "I just can't believe how sweet you are to each other. You know what? I'm gonna go home and I'm gonna be nicer to my husband."

"Well, I think that's a great idea," I said.

The stories I share at Trunk Shows aren't usually about such personal things. But when you talk to people in the audience, you can't help but open up sometimes. And if I can say something that might help someone, I'm glad to do it. Like the time I found myself struggling with some negative self-talk. I stood in front of a mirror before one of those shows and felt discouraged because I felt I was too overweight, I was too old, and I felt really sad about it.

For some reason, on that day, I went out in front of that audience and I told them exactly the way I was feeling. And so many of those women kept nodding their heads, as if they felt the very same thing.

"But then," I said, "this thought came into my mind: There are all these quilters out there who love you!"

That's when I told them about the positive self-talk that filled me up before I walked out on that stage: "You should love you," I said. "Your husband loves you. Your family loves you. They love you just how you are. And you should love you just how you are."

The audience applauded and cheered, and I know that applause wasn't for me as much as it was for each other.

**HERE'S WHAT HAPPENS** when you make a quilt—and more importantly, what happens when you give one away.

Let's say you give a quilt to somebody who has been diagnosed with cancer. They are going to feel the love. They'll feel all the hope. They'll feel everything you wanted them to feel. But what they're not going to know is that chemotherapy is cold. And when they go in for treatment, they are going to be wrapped in that warmth, and they didn't even know they needed that. It's a gift that gives them much more than they ever expected.

Let's say you make a quilt for your local sheriff to carry in the trunk of his car, so he can give it to a foster kid who needs help. When the sheriff picks up a foster kid, say a nine-year-old boy, and they pull him out of a home to go somewhere else, he's not necessarily going to feel love. He's likely going to be angry. And when the sheriff wraps him in that quilt, he's not going to say how beautiful it is or anything like that. But he might say, "Is it mine? Can I keep it?" Because everything he owns is now in a pillowcase, or a trash bag. And he might keep that quilt for the rest of his life—because it's *his*.

You never know how a quilt will be received. Everyone receives them differently.

Now, let's say you make a quilt for your son-in-law—maybe a son-in-law that you never really liked to begin with. And he and your daughter are now getting a divorce. On the way out of the house, he might give that quilt to Goodwill. That's okay, because guess what happens next? Somebody else finds that quilt, and says, "Oh my gosh, I can't believe I found this!" And that quilt you made is going to start a whole new life in somebody else's hands.

Quilts have the potential to outlive you by generations. You don't have to worry about the life they live, or what you had planned for them. They'll find their way. Quilts, like children, may not lead the life you intended, but trust me, they will find a path—and chances are, they'll change lives as they do.

Whether at Trunk Shows or quilting retreats, or back home in downtown Hamilton where more and more people were coming to visit our shops in person, people kept stopping to tell me, "Every morning I get up and I turn on one of your videos." And I always stopped to take that in, because I realized what that meant to them.

Even though I had never met these people, and even though they had never actually met me until that moment, I started to understand. And I responded: "So, you and I have spent some time together."

People told me that when they couldn't sleep, they watched the tutorials, and if they didn't feel good, they would watch the tutorials. And I started to realize that there was something about the connection of sharing quilting together online that healed people; that let people feel I was their friend, in their house, and we were buddies, and we quilted together. And no matter how many times I speak in front of audiences, large ones or small ones, even one-on-one, the real magic happens after I stop talking and start listening.

When one of my talks is over, it always surprises me when nearly everyone in the room lines up to shake my hand, or give me a hug, and every one of them wants to tell me their story. Sometimes meeting and greeting everyone goes on longer than my talks!

And almost every time, someone in that line brings me to tears.

Like the time there was a man who had stood in line for a very long time. He was all by himself, and he came to me and said, "My wife has Alzheimer's. And she's had Alzheimer's now for about five years, and she *loved* you. She loves quilting."

I was taken aback. I had worked with people with Alzheimer's and knew just how tactile they could be. There's a whole subset of quilters who make blankets called *fidget blankets*, with little tags, and silky sections, and rough sections, made especially for them.

But the man didn't ask me about those.

He said, "She hasn't spoken for many years, but she shuffles cards all the time. She just sits and shuffles. She and I never played cards together, so I don't really understand this whole card deal, but one day I decided to give her a deck of quilting cards. You know you have a deck of cards, right?"

"Yes," I said.

The playing cards he was referring to are part of a line of MSQC keepsakes and memorabilia that are sold in the Hamilton shops, and online. And those cards feature pictures of quilts—along with one card that has a picture of me on it.

"Do you know you're the Joker?" he asked me.

"Yes, I do know that," I said with a laugh. "My children did that to me."

He chuckled and said, "Well, my wife is shuffling through these cards, and all of a sudden it catches her eye that there are quilts on them, and she slows down, and she comes to the Joker card and she stops, and she looks at that card and looks at that picture of you," he said, "and then she looked up at me and said, 'It's Jenny.'"

At this point he had tears in his eyes—and so did I.

"Like I said," he continued, weeping at this point, "she hadn't spoken. For *years*. Do you know what it meant to me for one *moment* to know that my wife was still in there?"

The man gave me a great big bear hug and I thought, *holy smoke*. After hearing a story like that, I just wanted to lie down on the floor and have a good cry.

At another event, there was a woman in line who approached me with a baby strapped to her chest. "My baby has sensory issues," she said. "I can't put him down. If he's off my body, he literally goes into seizures. From the time he was born, I've worn him strapped to my body. I shower with him. I *sleep* with him."

I had never heard of anything like that happening with a child, so I started asking questions—and I noticed that every time I spoke, this woman's baby looked right at me.

"Every night I get in bed," the woman said, "and I think, *This is not the life I planned. This is a much harder life than I ever thought I'd have.*"

The fact that she had turned to quilting under such circumstances didn't surprise me, but I was surprised by what she said next: "You get me through those long nights, Jenny. I watch your tutorials all night long, and you've *saved* me. You get me through it."

"I don't know what to say," I replied. "I'm just so grateful that I've been able to help in some way."

I watched the baby as I spoke those words, and once again, it seemed clear to me that he knew my voice.

"I think he recognizes me," I said.

"Well, he hears you every single night," the woman said.

"Hello there," I said, and I smiled, and I held out my hands, and wouldn't you know it, that baby came right to me. He let me hold him—and his mother put her hands to her face and sobbed.

"No one has *ever* held him," she sobbed. "No one has ever held this baby but *me*."

Is that not the sweetest thing?

———

A year or so before most of the world went into its COVID-19 quarantine, Natalie, Misty, and I began offering what we call Doan Girls' Retreats, multi-day tutorial sessions led by us girls. And at one of these retreats with about a hundred mostly older women in attendance, there was one girl who seemed quite young compared to the rest of the group. She was very quiet, but one day, in private, she came up to me and she shared her story.

When she finished, I said to her, "I would love for you to share this story with everybody. I think it would be the most inspirational thing."

She was almost shocked that I would even suggest it.

"I'm just not sure I can," she said hesitantly.

"I think if you share this, you'll be amazed at the love that is in this room for you," I said, "and how unburdened you might feel—because when you share this, you don't know who else you're helping."

Later that week, we had a show-and-tell and I was about to start sharing one of my Trunk Show stories when the young woman looked at me, and she nodded, and I knew that in that moment, somehow she had found her courage. So I stopped talking and said to the group, "One of our retreaters here would like to share a story with you!"

She came up front and I went to take a seat, but she said, "Please don't leave me." So, I stood right there next to her to lend her my support as she spoke.

"I lost my home. I lost my family. I lost my children. I've been in jail more times than I can count," she said. At first, I wasn't sure if the audience knew what to make of this very nervous, pierced-up, tattooed girl who was now standing in front of them. But the more she spoke, the more love you could feel in that room.

"I had never been in trouble before. I had a good job. I worked for a doctor. I owned my own home and my cars were paid off. And I had tried some different drugs, but I was never addicted to anything until I made the biggest mistake of my life: I tried meth, and I was instantly addicted. I mean . . . when I couldn't get it, I would do whatever it took until I got what I needed.

"I was in and out of jail for the next four years. I barely saw my children for the next *six years*," she said. "I lost my job. I lost . . . everything. I was homeless. I didn't even own a hairbrush when I hit rock bottom.

"I came home because my grandmother, who was the only one who would speak to me, sent me twenty dollars and told me if I got on the bus, I could stay with her.

"Grandma was a quilter," she said. "She used to teach me to sew during summer visits, and give me tips and advice over the phone. I made my first quilt back in 1998, and I immediately fell in love with it. But I stopped doing that too. I didn't have a sewing machine, and my grandmother didn't have a working sewing machine in the last few years, either.

"Anyway . . . I got on the bus," she said. "I traveled eighteen-hundred miles across the country, and I took care of my grandma. And my grandma took care of me.

"She helped me get back on my feet. She loved me until I loved myself. She pushed me to rebuild my life, and I got a part-time job that became a full-time job, and I stayed *clean*," she said. "It was just a couple of years, though, when my grandma got real sick with cancer," she said. "She died in January of this year."

She paused to hold back her tears, and I don't think there was a dry eye in the whole room.

"I am just so grateful for everything she did for me. I've been clean for nearly six years now. I reconnected with my kids. My relationship with them is so strong now. And to honor my grandma, I decided it was time to do something I really loved, so I went out a few months ago and got myself a Bernina," she said. (That's a sewing machine.) "I remembered what Grandma had taught me, and I watched Jenny on YouTube, and I made my first quilt in nearly eleven years. I haven't stopped. Quilting is what's been getting me through ever since."

When she finished speaking, all of those women got up from their chairs and went to her, to wrap her up in their arms and share their love and encouragement.

And to think, when all of this started, I thought quilting was just for "old people."

I thought quilting was just a hobby.

# Small Town, Big Family

As much as my teaching has been life-changing for others, and all of this has been life-changing for me and our family, the growth of Missouri Star has been life-changing for the people of Hamilton and the surrounding towns too.

We have more than 450 employees on staff now. That's a lot of jobs in a rural area. And those employees are like one big hardworking family too. Our shipping is quick. Our social media and marketing and customer service teams are some of the best in any business. We have amazing creative and educational teams that make us all look good. We have machine-quilting and sewing teams that work on hundreds and hundreds of projects each week. And even further behind the scenes we have an HR team, a finance team, an operations team, a receiving and inventory management team, a product-buying team, a private-label team, and a construction/maintenance crew, which means Ron and Seth don't have to wear out their hands and knees in our buildings anymore.

That's on top of our wonderful retail team on the sales floors. We have thirteen quilt shops in downtown Hamilton now. People call it a Disneyland for Quilters. Before the pandemic, we were drawing 100,000 visitors per year to our shops—to a town of 1,500 people. We grew so big and so fast that teams from Google and YouTube and other big Silicon Valley companies have come out to interview us, just to hear our story and understand how to work with us. And just as I was finishing up the writing of this book, we were getting ready to reopen the shops—finally—after being closed for nearly a year.

When the stores are all open, downtown Hamilton is all hustle and bustle, full of laughing, happy people, and it's just the best. We're able to help other people's businesses thrive, and we love that. In the past few years we've had new restaurants come to town. Some nice folks built an event center in town. The hotels in the towns beyond Hamilton have seen their rooms sell out. Bus companies have increased business, catering to quilting guilds who want to come visit us all together. Our young chiropractor thanks us whenever Ron and I come in, because when she went off to college, she never expected she would be able to pursue her career in Hamilton. "Because of you guys, I'm able to have a job in my hometown," she says.

Even the Amish who bring pies and flowers to the center of town by horse and buggy have seen their sales double and triple.

I'll admit to having some real fun being the local *sew*-lebrity too. (I can't call myself a *celebrity*, because I'm not famous everywhere. I'm famous in this sewing-circle world of quilting. So a *sew*-lebrity is what I am!)

Like the time I noticed an older gentleman sitting on the bench in front of our main shop. He looked bored, as if he had been waiting on someone for a long time, so I went up to him and said, "Is your wife in there shopping?"

"Yeah," he said.

"Why don't you scoot over?" I asked him. "Let's take a picture and send it to her."

"Why would I do that?" he asked.

"Just trust me on this."

I sat down, he reluctantly took this selfie, and I said, "Now send it to your wife." I stood up and gave him some space, and thirty seconds later the door of the shop flew open and she came running out saying, "Where is she? Where'd she go?"

She spotted me and got all excited. "Oh! Can I give you a hug?"

"Sure!" I said.

Her husband looked at me puzzled and said, "Who *are* you?"

"Oh, come on!" his wife said as we took a selfie for her too. "How could you not know? It's Jenny!"

People need to have fun, and want to have fun. And because I love to have fun, too, a few years after we opened we decided to throw our first MSQC Birthday Bash. We promised we'd have hot dogs, and music, and raffles and giveaways, and we invited customers and neighbors and some of our suppliers and salespeople to come celebrate with us at the shop.

We anticipated we'd get maybe twenty or thirty people to show up that weekend, so Ron went overboard. He went out and bought fifty hot dogs and set up the grill outside in the vacant lot next door, which is right in the center of downtown Hamilton. We blew up balloons and put up streamers and made sure the shop was in tip-top shape. And no sooner did we open than the people started streaming in from all over. Every parking space in town was filled before noon! There were *hundreds* of people. Ron had to run to the local supermarket up the street and buy more hot dogs. And an hour later he had to run up there again and buy every last hot dog they had.

The shop was so packed, I was glad I was tall. The only way I could talk to our employees, or Alan or Natalie or Sarah, or Bernice and Delores (who showed up to help too) was to shout over the tops of all the customers' heads!

There wasn't a restaurant in town back then. There was hardly anything for any of these visitors to do except to buy things in our store and eat Ron's hot dogs. But for some reason, everybody had big smiles on their faces. My cheeks hurt by the end of the day after posing for what felt like a million selfies with customers who had come from near and far to see the shop and meet me in person. We were so overwhelmed by it all.

The next year we planned for an even bigger crowd, and a bigger crowd is what we got. There were close to a thousand people there. We organized a stage with music outside, and we held a Layer-Cake Walk, like an old-fashioned cake walk. Participants had to step up when their number was called and give us their best "walk," which was code for showing off some dance moves, with the best dancer earning a cake. Only in this case, our winners got a Fabric Layer Cake, which is a collection of ten-inch fabric squares all stacked up so they sort of look like the layers of a little ol' cake. And you should have seen it! We had ladies out there kicking up their heels and dancing like their lives depended on it, all to win one of these prizes. There were women in wheelchairs and scooters who couldn't dance who convinced their husbands to get out there and dance for them. And the husbands obliged! And when they won a prize, these women went scooting around in a victory lap with the layer cake in their laps.

Just like you would see at a kids' birthday party, we put up a big piñata. Only this piñata was filled with quilting supplies, and it was hilarious to see how hard these ladies would swing that stick in the hopes of breaking it open.

It was so much fun to see so many people smiling and laughing and having fun, all because of our little quilt shop.

At one point I got up on the makeshift stage and went to the microphone and asked where everybody was from, and people started shouting: "We came all the way from Texas!" "Kansas City!" "Washington, DC!"

Then someone yelled out, "France!" Then, "England!"

It brought tears to my eyes. How was this possible? How were we reaching people from so far away? And why were they willing to come all this way to visit this little quilt shop in the middle of Missouri?

"Gallatin!" someone shouted, and I laughed. Gallatin's located just a few minutes north of where we were standing.

"Across the street!" a local business owner yelled, and everyone laughed at that one.

"Well, thanks for walking all five steps to get here," I said. "But truly, thank you. Thanks to every one of you."

I looked around at my children, and over at Ron, as he smiled and shook his head in awe. "We are all so grateful you're here."

Toward the end of one of our most recent Birthday Bashes, Alan came up to me and asked, "Mom, what was the best part of your day?"

I love that question. Hearing it from my grown kids after asking them when they were little for so many years makes it so special.

I thought about it as I looked up at him, and then at all my kids, and at all the people who were there to celebrate with us, and I said, "The best part of my day? The best part of my day is seeing all of these smiling faces, and knowing that we're making a difference."

My kids and Ron and I all shared a big group bear hug, as the sounds of music and families full of laughter bounced off the old brick walls of our beautiful little town.

Our whole extended family joins in the fun and gets involved with the preparations for the Birthday Bash celebrations every year now, and most of the fabric companies and distributors we work with send representatives and offer prizes and giveaways, too, because they've come to love our customers and our company.

Isn't that *something*?

By doing something I love doing, and by listening to my grown children's advice, and by working together as a family, we are now in the business of bringing people *together*—hundreds, even thousands of people, not only from our town, but from all over the world, and from all different walks of life—all in the name of love and joy and creativity.

———

People often ask me what all of this success has meant to me, personally. And my answer is, "Well, for the first time in my life, I can walk into a grocery store and buy whatever I want without having to worry about it." That's a *huge* change for me after decades of raising seven children on a very limited budget. It was almost hard to get used to at first.

Walking through a grocery store as a *sew*-lebrity is something new too. Sometimes Ron will be behind me and hear people whisper, "Is that Jenny? I think maybe that's Jenny Doan!" and he'll joke with them: "Do you want to get a picture? Because I can make that happen!"

"Wait . . . Oh my gosh, you're Mr. Jenny!" they'll shout, and we'll stop and pose for selfies, and it's still so amazing to think that perfect strangers value what we do.

And, as any mother would understand, it is also so wonderful to know that my children are prospering—not just because our business is doing well, but because they're touching people's lives in positive ways too.

It can be overwhelming at times. I can't help but ask God sometimes, "Why me? Why do *I* get to do this? Why am *I* the vehicle?"

My whole life I tried to do what I loved, and to share love with the people around me. Being a mom, teaching, sewing, making the best of whatever we had, figuring things out and having fun while we did it—those are the same things I'm still doing every day. But by working together, Ron and I somehow managed to create this family that also learned to figure things out, and to have fun while we did it, and that believes in each other in ways that would take all of us to places we never dreamed we could go.

I don't spend a lot of time thinking about these things. I don't spend a lot of time making plans for the future, either. I live mostly in the here and now, and always have. But in the rare moments when my mind will wander over all of it, I am so grateful for all of the grace, for all the people who have helped us along the way, and for all of the little blessings that God has provided us—so many little blessings that added up to a whole lot, for a family that didn't have a ton.

What I realize now is the pieces of all of our lives are being stitched together. The fabric stretches all the way back to our mothers and fathers, and grandmothers and grandfathers. In my case it went all the way back to my great-great grandmother and her daughters, the seamstresses, who helped bring my grandmother to America. But in all of our lives, so many of the little pieces of our past are part of the beautiful quilt that tells our story. A quilt that can warm us and comfort us if we are willing to reach for it.

While many of our stories are fraught with heartache and hardship, what I've learned is that they are also filled with the batting of blessings—bound with dedication, hard work, faith, and, above all else, love for one another. And sometimes, even when we're not aware of it, it's all of that love and dedication that gets passed down to the generations that come after us.

I see evidence of it all the time, especially in my own grandkids.

At Christmastime with a family as big as ours, we draw names. And it was not long ago when my twelve-year-old granddaughter, Alayna, one of Hillary's daughters, drew my name out of the hat.

I didn't know it at the time, but this granddaughter of mine had decided she wanted to do something really special for me that Christmas: she wanted to make me a quilt. People usually don't make quilters quilts, but that's what she wanted to do. So she sent a letter to all of my grandchildren, and asked them to trace their hands on paper. Then she cut out fabric in the shape of each of those little hands and sewed every one of them on a tree that she had designed in the middle of the quilt.

When I opened it, and I saw what she had done, I wept.

Her quilt was covered with all of the colorful handprints of each one of my grandchildren, and right in the middle of the tree trunk she had hand-embroidered a heart, with "R + J" in the middle of it, as if it was etched in the tree.

"This is the sweetest thing," I said to her through joy-filled tears. "I mean, it's just absolutely the sweetest thing. I'm going to hang it on my wall so I can look at it every day."

"Oh, Grandma," she said. "No! I want you to wrap up in it. I want you to put it around you!"

As she came over and gently wrapped our shoulders in that beautiful quilt, I looked over at Ron, and I looked around at this beautiful family we'd made, and I looked back at my grand-daughter and pulled her in for a great big hug, and I nodded.

"All right, then," I said. "I will."

# Afterword

With the shops reopened and life beginning to return to normal as this book goes to print in 2021, I thought it might be nice to give everyone a little update on the current lives of our family members.

Darrell and his wife, Stephanie, are living in California now. They have two boys and are busy with all that life brings. Darrell works in urban development, and Stephanie is a food chemist.

Natalie lives in Hamilton. She has five children, a daughter-in-law, a son-in-law, and two dogs. She has done just about every job in the company. She is currently the editor of *Block* magazine. She designs many of the quilt patterns that we teach on YouTube and teaches with me on Triple Play tutorials. Natalie also has a show called *Final Stitch*, and her daughter Hannah works for us in social media.

Sarah and her husband, Seth, live in Hamilton. They also have five children. Sarah has always been passionate about our company, and although she has stepped back from her daily roles to focus on her family, she and Seth are still very involved in the care and development of our town. Three of her children work for us: Annie in marketing, and Katie and Ella do whatever we need but are currently playing our mascots, Chuck the Duck and Princess Patchwork.

Hillary lives in Arkansas with her husband, Alex, and their five children. She is talented in so many ways, but especially loves to write. She has published a couple of novels and runs an annual writing conference. She is currently writing the much-loved mystery story for *Block* magazine.

Alan and his wife, Drea, have three little boys and are living twenty miles outside of Hamilton. Alan has now stepped back from his daily role in our company and is working on a few new business ideas. He loves the entrepreneur life. He still pops in to make sure things are going along smoothly. He is loving life spending time with his family on his little farm.

Jacob and his wife, Misty, live in Hamilton with their three children. Jacob has spent the last ten years carefully crafting the image of Missouri Star in message and video. He has also stepped back from his daily role in the film studio. He loves to spend time with his family and especially loves to landscape his yard. Misty is currently the host of *Missouri Star Live* each week on Facebook. She also teaches quilting with me on Triple Play week.

Josh lives here in Hamilton. He has one son, who he loves to spend time with. He has always loved helping people and is currently working in our customer service department.

Then there is Ron and I. We are still here, plugging along. Happy to be here in this moment. Happy to be surrounded by our family and loved ones. Happy to have jobs we love and things to do that matter.

And *everything* matters.

# Acknowledgments

Boy, has this been a journey, and like any journey, it wouldn't be complete without the help of others.

I would like to thank my parents, my siblings, and all those who came before, whose stories molded my story.

I would like to thank my family. I have a family unlike any other, and they rally around to help and encourage in any way they can. They give hope to the human heart that there is good in the world. I would like to thank my children, Darrell, Natalie, Sarah, Hillary, Alan, Jacob, and Joshua, for loving me, and for putting up with all my crazy ideas. For letting me be a fun mom and for knowing that even though every day wasn't perfect, we did the best we could . . . always.

I would like to thank my husband, Ron, for his complete love and incredible support. I have in him a stellar man whose love knows no bounds. He sees me.

I would like to thank my daughter Hillary for helping me navigate this world I knew nothing about. For her late-night computer help and never being too busy to listen to her mom. I would like to thank my daughter Natalie for lending her incredible intellectual way of thinking. She can somehow cross the bridge to my scattered brain and put order to everything.

# Acknowledgments

I would like to thank my daughter-in-law Misty and my friend Cherry, who took time to read and share their honest opinions with me.

I would like to thank Mark Dagostino and Terry Taylor for their willingness to listen, to travel, to hear and understand the feelings of my heart, and to put it all down on paper. What a gift to be able to tell others' stories.

I would like to thank Andrea Fleck-Nisbet, Amanda Bauch, John Andrade, and the entire team at Harper Horizon, Jeff Farr at Neuwirth & Associates, and Mollie Glick at CAA, for believing in me and my story, and seeing a story worth telling. And of course, thanks to everyone at MSQC—and all of the loyal fans and customers of MSQC—for showing so much love to my family and for our story, from the start.

Lastly, I would like to give special thanks to Al and Sarah, who convinced me and enabled us to start the Missouri Star Quilt Company in the first place. Especially Al, who, like me, sees adventure everywhere and whose loving and persuasive nature has been the moving force behind this book and so much of our company's growth. Without his tenacious personality, I would still be in that corner shop!

# Recipes

## Doans' Big Batch Cookies

These are the cookies we made to feed lots and lots of mouths!
Be warned: it'll take you a long time to get these all in and out
of the oven. The note on the bottom of my recipe card says,
"Bake all night!" But if you don't want to bake this many all at
once, this dough can be rolled up in plastic wrap and frozen, so
you'll have ready-to-go dough in the freezer. This recipe pro-
vides a base for chocolate chips, raisins, nuts, peanut butter, or
almost anything else you want to add. Mix it up and have fun
with it!

*Makes approximately 16 dozen*

2 cups shortening

2 cups (4 sticks) butter, softened

4 cups (28 ounces) granulated
   sugar

4 cups (24 ounces) firmly
   packed brown sugar

8 eggs

4 teaspoons vanilla extract

7 ½ cups all-purpose flour

4 teaspoons baking soda

4 teaspoons salt

6 cups rolled oats

1 large package of chocolate
   chips, optional

2 cups raisins, optional

2 cups chopped nuts, optional

1. Preheat the oven to 350°F. Grease cookie sheets with shortening, butter, or cooking spray.
2. In a large bowl, cream together the shortening, butter, sugar, brown sugar, eggs, and vanilla.
3. Add the flour, baking soda, salt, and oats and mix well to combine.
4. If you like, stir in chocolate chips, raisins, and/or nuts.
5. Drop the dough by spoonfuls onto the prepared cookie sheets. Bake for 8 to 10 minutes, until golden brown. Remove from the oven, allow the cookies to cool for a couple of minutes, then take them off the sheets.
6. Add spoonfuls of dough to those same cookie sheets and bake additional batches into the oven, until you have the desired number of cookies. (No need to re-grease the cookie sheets in between batches.)
7. Enjoy with some ice-cold milk!

# Buttermilk Chocolate Cake

This is my mother's recipe—the one Ron fell in love with the first time he came over to visit.

*Makes one 11x17-inch sheet cake*

Butter, for greasing pan
2 cups all-purpose flour
2 cups granulated sugar
1 teaspoon baking soda
1 teaspoon cinnamon
1 cup (2 sticks) butter
¼ cup (4 tablespoons) cocoa powder
1 cup water
½ cup buttermilk
2 eggs

1 teaspoon vanilla extract

FROSTING
½ cup (1 stick) butter
⅓ cup (6 tablespoons) milk
¼ cup cocoa powder
1 16-ounce box (4 cups) powdered sugar
½ teaspoon vanilla extract
1 cup chopped nuts, optional

1. Preheat the oven to 400°F. Grease an 11x17-inch baking pan with butter or nonstick cooking spray.
2. In a large bowl, mix together the flour, sugar, baking soda, and cinnamon.
3. In a medium saucepan, combine the butter, cocoa, and water, and bring to a rapid boil. Pour the mixture into the mixing bowl with the dry ingredients and stir well.
4. Add the buttermilk, eggs, and vanilla to the large bowl and mix well.
5. Scrape the batter into the prepared pan. Bake for 15 to 18 minutes, until a toothpick inserted in the middle of the cake comes out clean and/or the cake begins to pull a bit away from the edges.

6. For the frosting: In a medium saucepan, bring the butter, milk, and cocoa to a boil. Remove from the heat, add the powdered sugar and vanilla and stir to combine.

7. Frost the cake while it is still warm and top with the nuts of your choice (maybe half with nuts, half without. Get crazy—it's your cake!).

# Frosty Strawberry Squares

This was my winning entry in one of our very first Doansbury Bake-Offs.

*Makes 12 squares*

CRUST
1 cup all-purpose flour
¼ cup packed brown sugar
½ cup (1 stick) butter
½ cup walnuts

FILLING
2 cups sliced fresh strawberries

or 1 (10-ounce) box thawed
frozen strawberries, plus
more for garnish
⅔ cup granulated sugar
2 egg whites
2 tablespoons lemon juice
1 cup whipped cream or
Cool Whip

1. Preheat the oven to 350°F.
2. For the crust: In a large bowl, mix together the flour, brown sugar, butter, and walnuts, then spread on a cookie sheet. Bake for 15 minutes until the mixture is toasted, stirring occasionally so it doesn't burn.
3. Sprinkle ⅔ of the crust crumbs in a 9x13-inch baking pan.
4. For the filling: In a large bowl, combine the strawberries, sugar, egg whites, and lemon juice. Mix with an electric mixer until stiff peaks form, about 10 minutes. Add the whipped cream or Cool Whip and gently stir it into the berry filling.
5. Evenly spread the filling over the crust in the pan, then top with the remaining ⅓ of the crumbs. Cover and freeze for 6 hours or overnight.
6. Garnish with whole berries and serve cold.

# About the Authors

JENNY DOAN is the cofounder and face of Missouri Star Quilt Company. Quilting is a journey she began as an adult, after moving to small-town Hamilton, Missouri, and looking for a new creative outlet. After one class, she was hooked and began sharing her new passion with family and friends. A lifelong learner and natural encourager, Jenny now teaches millions of viewers how to make beautiful quilts by breaking down the process into easy steps. Jenny's humor and can-do mindset have helped people around the world learn to quilt and believe that they can do it. You can join her every Friday morning on YouTube for a fresh new quilting project. When she's not quilting, she loves traveling, hiking, gardening, reading, and crafting. Her advice for new quilters? "Don't be afraid to try! Everything is a learned skill. If you sew an hour today, tomorrow you will be an hour better."

MARK DAGOSTINO is a multiple *New York Times* bestselling co-author who is dedicated to writing books that uplift and inspire.